John W. Drakeford

Experiential Bible Study

Broadman Press/Nashville, Tennessee

© Copyright 1974—Broadman Press
Nashville, Tennessee
All rights reserved
4219-30
ISBN: 0-8054-1930-6

Dewey Decimal Classification: 220.07
Library of Congress Catalog Card Number: 74-80338
Printed in the United States of America

To Robina
who practices the psychology
I teach

Preface

For over twenty years I have tried to teach psychology, and I enjoy every moment of it. Human motivations, behavior, and maladjustment have all fascinated me. The books I've been privileged to write have been in this fruitful area.

In this volume I return to my first love—the Bible. I have long grappled with the problems of reconciling much psychological theory with the biblical revelation, but, having watched psychological fads come and go, I find it refreshing to return to the timeless message of the Bible.

However, I am troubled by the way in which the Bible is taught. We use such slipshod methods to handle such priceless truths.

When as a new Christian I first attended Bible study meetings, they were held in a home. We sat and listened to a teacher who held forth on some biblical theme. It did little for me. My most vivid memory is of a cute girl, whom I used to walk home after the meeting.

That girl became my wife, and it is appropriate that she and I working as a husband-wife team should have produced the method which we now call Experiential Bible Study.

Robina, my wife, already widely experienced in our Integrity Therapy groups, became the foremost exponent of Experiential Bible Study. As I produced the programs, she put them into practice.

Traveling across the country in our Family Enrichment Programs, Robina has used this technique with remarkable results, and we offer these programs to those blessed people—Bible teachers—with a prayer that this technique may provide many fruitful experiences.

JOHN W. DRAKEFORD

Contents

PART I
The Foundations of Experiential Bible Study

1

Spectators or Participators?

What do football and contemporary Christianity have in common? They have both fostered the spectator idea.

In the realm of sports we have changed from participators to spectators. Television has fostered the process that lets us have our exercise vicariously. Doctors worry about overfed and under-exercised Americans digging their graves with their knives and forks, while sitting and watching paid professionals provide them with the thrill of conflict. These authorities urge upon Americans, "Get out and participate. Otherwise, sporting events will accomplish nothing for you."

Contemporary Christianity is beset by the same problems, as we have turned into a generation of spectator Christians.

Returning from a tour of Europe, I felt in hearty accord with a fellow traveler who, after an unrelieved diet of cathedrals and sundry other samples of ecclesiastical architecture, remarked, "I don't care if I never see another church."

Of course, he was using the word "church" in the colloquial and inaccurate sense of referring to a building rather than to a body of believers; and he meant he was sick of gloomy buildings in which a handful of worshipers had come—and not over reverently—to watch a spectacle that would be acted out on the altar in front of them.

However, one German church building interested me. A beautiful stone chapel perched high on the mountaintop, it looks down on the valley, deep below, where nestles the tiny town of Weschnitz.

The trees have been cut from the mountainside forest to allow a winding pathway, like some enormous aisle, to be built from the valley below to the church. After climbing that precipitous trail, I anticipated entering the church, not so much to worship God as to sprawl on one of the seats and relax and recuperate my spent energies.

Alas for my hopes. The seats in the chapel were simple affairs with four legs and no backs on them. No chance of rest or relaxation here.

The same situation exists in the historic New Room, the church built by John Wesley in Bristol, where the original pews are similarly without backs. Any unfortunate worshiper who nodded off during a church service there would be in peril of falling from the seat and damaging his neck.

Modern churches have looked after this problem by providing comfortable cushioned pews to give the attendees an easy resting place. Small wonder that one comfortable worshiper was able to write:

> I never see my preacher's eyes,
> No matter how bright they shine.
> When he prays he shuts them tight.
> When he preaches he closes mine.

The shape of church buildings has encouraged the spectator idea. Most church buildings are rectangular—long, narrow-gutted affairs that seat the members in the same type of row arrangement that they would encounter in attending the movies or a play to be presented on the stage in front of them.

As the churchgoers enter the building, they immediately commence to act out their spectator role by filling the auditorium from the rear. They may even take a peculiar pride in the fact that they are getting as far away from the action as they can. Hence, the comment by someone who has resisted every effort to cajole him into a seat near the front of the building, and who proudly remarks, "We're good Baptists."

In such a situation I have felt a deep compulsion to respond, "You're not good Baptists. You are sorry Baptists, spectator Baptists."

The situation is further aggravated when an "outsider" wanders into the service and discovers there is no possibility of just "slipping into a back seat," because the only vacant seats are at the very front of the church. The church members have filled the safe and secure back seats in a solid block so that they can sit and *observe* what is going on. If they are particularly devout, they may follow the outsider's progress with interest, and even pray for him as he hesitatingly takes tentative steps to the "no man's land" in the front of the church building.

Once the church service is underway, the chance visitor may discover that the music of the service is also aimed at the spectator effort. The elaborately gowned choir, full-time professional music director, expensive organ are all part of the performance. When it comes to congregational singing, he is supplied with an elaborate hymnal with all the music before him, but he discovers that only a small proportion of the people sing, while most of them gaze into space as if in hope of espying some unidentified flying object, their countenances bringing the nonverbal message of "not here."

This book is an effort to sell Christians on an idea: quit being a spectator and participate, particularly in the area of Bible study.

No other single book has ever been studied so diligently, by so many people, as has the Bible, and a great variety of methods of study has been introduced. Despite all this effort few people are happy about these techniques. This book is an effort to promote another technique—studying the Bible *experientially.*

The Bible is many things.

The Bible is history. Contained within its pages are some of the oldest documents known to mankind.

The Bible is literature. One of the best received courses in the English department of one large university is "The English Bible As Literature," and in this thoroughly secularized university the Bible is viewed as appropriate material for literary studies.

The Bible is poetry. Even though poetry loses much in the translation from one language to another, great poetic passages of the Old and, to a lesser degree, the New Testament retain their poetic impact.

The Bible is singing. Songs sung down through the centuries are part of the Bible. One portion of it, the book of Psalms, is composed of a large number of significant songs.

Preeminently, the Bible is *experience*. It tells of the experiences of Israel in her fluctuating relationships with God, and relates the story of the birth, growth, and development of the Christian church. In the course of these stories it inevitably focuses on individuals and their experiences with both God and man.

The Bible zeros in on an individual's experience. Whatever it tells of spectator religion, it condemns.

Most methods of Bible study have placed the would-be student in the spectator role. He is a bystander who listens while his teacher holds forth on features of the passage being taught. But if this book is a volume of experiences, it follows that it will be most profitable to study it experientially.

The word "experience" comes from the Latin *experior* which means "to test or try." The distinguished theologian Strong says, "Experience is the teaching and proving of truth objectively contained in God's revelation." Experiential Bible Study is an effort to encourage the individual to apply biblical truths to his human experience.

Martin Luther certainly practiced this, as his actions at the Marburg Colloquy attest. This conference was held in Philip of Hesse's castle, which still stands today, dramatically perched on an elevated spot overlooking the towered German city of Marburg. Visitors enter the castle, having ascended the steep road up the hillside, only to wander through long hallways before at last reaching the room in which the celebrated Colloquy was held.

In this historic room, at the urging of Philip of Hesse, a group of Reformation leaders met to see if they could resolve their doctrinal differences and present a common statement of faith to the world of their day. The two leading figures in the discussion were Martin Luther, the German, and Ulrich Zwingli, the Swiss reformer. They agreed upon ten points, but, when they came to the subject of communion, serious disagreements arose.

Martin Luther stated his position quite clearly when he drew a circle on the table—which may be seen to this very day—and within the circle wrote, "This is my body," and took his adamant stand upon the literal interpretation of these words.

The insistence on the literal meaning of this statement indicated the way in which Luther was rejecting many of the allegorizing methods of biblical interpretation that had been used by the medieval church.

Luther had been through the crucible of a struggle for faith. According to tradition, as he climbed the Scala Sancta in Rome— the twenty-eight steps said to have been located outside of Pilate's palace—repeating the Pater Noster and kissing each step for good measure, he finally jumped to his feet and asked, "Who knows whether this is so?" That question led him on a pathway of a quest for faith.

Disillusioned with the established church and its pronouncements, Luther had turned to the Bible for authority in belief and guidance in his spiritual pilgrimage. As this book became increasingly helpful to him, leading him to defy the authority of the church, he felt he should share it with the common people, in the hope that it would lead them into similar experiences. The manuscripts had been available to the scholars; now Luther sought to place the message into the hands of the common people. He translated the Bible into the German language so that all who wished could read.

But, as important as he knew reading to be, Luther realized his efforts must go further than this. In his own personal handling of the Bible, Luther interpreted it *experientially*. Commenting on his lectures on the book of Jonah, the historian Bainton says, "Luther handled Jonah as he did every other biblical character—as a mirror of his own experience." Luther, this man of action, realized there must be some process whereby the reader identified with what was taking place in the biblical story and made an application to his own personal life.

The idea of Experiential Bible Study is presented here as a new way of coming at understanding the Bible, but, in the light of Luther's experience, we might better describe it as the rediscovery of an old way of doing things.

It is to be hoped that studying the Bible experientially will help to deal a deathblow to spectator Christianity by making the message of the Bible a vital, motivating force in our modern twentieth-century living.

Sharing a similar experience of faith with Luther, a common resource with the Bible, and the same experiential method of studying the Divine Book, another Luther may be raised up, who will face the evils of our day, no longer willing to be a passive spectator but declaring with his predecessor, "Here I stand—so help me God."

2

Involvement:
The Pathway to
Self-Discovery

The best way to discover God is to realize the personal, distinctive nature of the experience, withdraw from the distracting voices of fellowmen, and seek an encounter in a solitary place.

Not if we believe John Wesley. He tried the lonely way.

He commenced his spiritual quest under the spell of the mystics. The great writers of classical, mystical literature, Thomas Kempis, Jeremy Taylor, and William Law, all influenced him, causing him to spend long hours in lonely vigils but all in vain.

At this critical moment in his spiritual quest John Wesley went to the Church of England church at Wroote to serve as the interim rector. While involved in this work, he heard about a godly man, the Rev. Hoole, vicar of the distant church of Haxey. Wesley undertook the journey to visit the vicar. While with him he poured out the story of his spiritual quest, and the vicar replied, "Sir, you wish to serve God and go to heaven? Remember that you cannot serve him alone. You must therefore find companions or make them; the Bible knows nothing of solitary religion."

A keen student of the Bible, Wesley came to see that, though the inspired writings occasionally tell of a Moses going into the desert or a Paul retreating to Arabia, the main thrust of the biblical revelation is to put people into group relationships with each other, and from which contact they come to experience God.

Wesley's quest went forward in experiences of relationship. At Oxford University he joined the Holy Club, a group of men who met to study, teach children, and minister to the unfortunates languishing in prison. When Wesley accepted the challenge of

Governor Oglethorpe to sail the Atlantic to Georgia, he set up a group consisting of himself, his brother Charles, and two others, Ingham and Delamotte. Before embarking on this enterprise, they entered into a compact that no one member of the group would make a major decision without consulting the other three. This provision was to deal Wesley his bitterest blow.

In Georgia, when he agonized over his relationship with Sophia Hopkey, he found his friends more than anxious to assist him in making his decision. Their simple solution, don't. But the original agreement provided that, if the group couldn't agree, they were to draw lots. So three statements were written: "Marry"; "Not this year"; "Think no more of it." When the lots was drawn, it turned out to be "Think no more of it."

Despite such a disappointing outcome of the group-decision making process, Wesley still believed in groups. After his return to England, he went on a trip to Germany to study the complex organizations of the Moravians. Upon his return he helped to found a new group, known as the Fetter Lane Society, where people gathered to "confess their faults one to another."

The Moravians continued to haunt Wesley. In America the Moravian Spangenburg had asked him difficult questions, such as "Do you know Jesus Christ?" and "Do you know he has saved you?" Now another Moravian, Peter Bohler, entered into serious discussion with Wesley about his spiritual condition, and the historian Tyerman says Bohler finally convinced Wesley of the importance of the "experience test" in gaining religious assurance.

And when the much-sought-after experience came, the great event took place in a group. Wesley describes the experience in his own words: "In the evening I went very unwillingly to a society in Aldersgate Street where one was reading Luther's preface to the Epistle to the Romans. At about a quarter before nine while he was describing the change which God works in the heart through faith in Christ, I felt my heart strangely warmed. I felt I did trust in Christ, Christ alone for salvation; and assurance was given me that he had taken away my sins, even mine, and saved me from the law of sin and death."

Balance may be one of the most needed notes in today's ministry.

The Rev. Harry Streetman felt as if God had issued him a peremptory summons to get out and work to take the message to lost men. After years of indifference to the things of the spirit, he went through a crisis illness and on recovery made his commitment to Christ and forthwith became an enthusiastic evangelist. In the fervor of his commitment he nursed a suspicion about his friend Bill Harris, who was at that time involved in a ministry in an underprivileged part of the city.

Bill Harris, for his part, majors on social work. He considers that the Christian gospel urges Christians to be concerned about the physical needs of the less fortunates of this world. In talking with Robert Vogel he often speculates about Harry Streetman's preoccupation with evangelism, and comments, "When a man is hungry, it's not much use talking to him about his soul. His body is too agonizingly real. Feed him, then he will be willing to listen."

While Robert Vogel partly agrees with Bill Harris on this matter, he is not so sure that Harris himself is going about things in the right way. Vogel has been through T-groups, sensitivity training, and a whole host of group techniques. He feels that anyone seeking to help another person must use some of these methods of developing human potential. He has grave questions about both Harris and Streetman.

The enthusiast is always tempted to feel that his method and his alone is the way to help people. By way of contrast, John Wesley, accused in his day of enthusiasm, had a sense of balance in his significant work. The three notes of *evangelism, social concerns,* and *small groups* stand out in his ministry.

Evangelism Following his "heartwarming" experience in the Aldersgate meeting, Wesley launched upon a tremendous evangelistic enterprise. His intensity antagonized many of the ministers of the established churches, and he took to the open air in a ministry of "field preaching." Wherever he could get with a group of people, he proclaimed the message of the evangel.

Social Concerns   Along with evangelism there went a concern for the bodies of men and women. Wesley established dispensaries, and he dabbled in medicine himself, writing a book called *Primitive Physic*, in which he offered remedies for the common illnesses of eighteenth-century Englishmen. He also inaugurated programs for establishing orphanages and schools, and schemes to help people improve their lot in life.

Small Groups   However, Wesley was preeminently the man of groups. Wesley stated his position, "Christianity is essentially a social religion, and to turn it into a solitary religion is to destroy it." In the preface to his first Methodist hymnbook in 1739 he took up the same idea: "The gospel of Christ knows no religion but social, no holiness but social holiness. This commandment have we from God that he who loves God love his brother also."

This conviction led Wesley to establish a unique system of small groups through which the eighteenth-century Methodist moved. These groups were the society, the class meeting, the band, and the select society. A Methodist began his experience by joining the *society*, in which the requirement was, to have a desire "to flee from the wrath to come." Later he moved into the *class meeting*, in which the discussion focused on the behavior of the participants during the previous week. The next challenge was to join the band, whose objective was for members to "confess your faults one to another." If this Methodist wished to aspire for the highest goal of all, he became a part of the *select society*, whose members aimed at perfection.

Surveying the intricate group organization and the requirements, it becomes clear that, for the Wesleyans, it was "by their experience shall ye know them." By emphasizing this mode, using groups based on affinity of similar experiences, Wesley may have been recapturing a lost biblical idea.

In the opening drama of the book of Genesis the penalty of Adam's sin is separation from God; and when a recalcitrant Cain was condemned to live as a fugitive and a vagabond, the thought of his isolation caused him to cry out. "My punishment is greater than I can bear." And later, in the dark days of the Hebrews in exile, "They that feared the Lord spoke oft one to another."

The note of union stands out particularly clearly in the New Testament. Jesus had a group of disciples who were with him, and within their ranks were degrees of closeness, beginning with an inner circle and moving out. In his moments of high spiritual experience Jesus took this inner circle to share them with him.

Questioned as to the greatest of all the commandments, Jesus allied himself with the Mosaic statement: "Thou shalt love the Lord thy God with all thy heart, with all thy soul, with all thy might, and with all thy strength." He immediately hastened to add, "And second is like unto it, thou shalt love thy neighbor as thyself." For Jesus the experiences were two sides of the same coin, and to him it seemed improbable that a man could love God and not consider his fellowman.

Following the death of Christ, one hundred twenty of his frightened followers gathered together "in one accord," and on the day of Pentecost "they were all with one accord in one place." Immediately after the Pentecostal effusion, Peter "stood up with the eleven" and declared the Pentecostal message with the result that three thousand people were added to the church, "and all that believed were together and had all things in common."

Wherever we look in the biblical record there are groups. People gathered for fellowship, relationship, association. These become key experiences of the biblical story.

Facing this situation, we realize that the Bible not only contains a message but also reveals a way of doing things. It sets forth a principle of human relationships in groups. A man discovered God and then went out to relate to his fellows; and the Bible tells us how he went about it.

Although the term "group dynamics" is of fairly recent origin, the experiences of grouping are as old as man himself. Groups have always been important in Christianity, and the New Testament portrays a heavy use of group techniques.

Rather unfortunately, the church doesn't always put a true estimate on its possessions. It sometimes wonders whether it is really keeping up to date and discards its techniques in favor of newer methods, only to discover that there are others standing by and waiting to seize discards and loudly proclaim them as new and innovative.

We are living in a day of small groups. Among the social scientists, social workers and psychotherapists have used them extensively. Industry has found tremendous values from small groups; and people in the living rooms of the nation gather in every type of group: sensitivity, discussion, Bible study, encounter, and a dozen others.

This volume is a call to Christians to return to the historic use of the group and enrich the process by wedding the techniques of the group to the all-important study of the Bible. To make the application obvious, we will consider in detail this new way of studying an old book.

3
The New Way
of Studying
an Old Book

Of all the books ever written, the Bible is the most widely sold and distributed—and the least read. And when people *do* get around to making a try at reading the Good Book, many of them find it dry and uninteresting. The result is, all the Bibles that are printed and sold are used for many purposes: for taking oaths; as presents for mothers of new babies; for carrying at weddings, for propping open the motel door, but for reading— that's another matter.

This book is written from the conviction that the Bible is a book—a book meant to be read and studied. The second half of this volume will present a series of programs utilizing the experiential method of studying the Bible in a way that will make the Bible relevant to the particular experiences through which we are passing in our everyday lives.

The Distinctives of Experiential Bible Study

Experiential Bible Study differs from the more commonly used types of Bible reading or study in at least five different ways:

1. *The Method Is Personal.* It calls for the individual to think about his own *personal* experiences and relate them to the Biblical passage, hence the title *Experiential Bible Study.* In many ways making the Bible apply to life is the crux of the problem we face today, and Experiential Bible Study gives us this opportunity.

2. *The Leader Functions Differently.* The leader's role is different. While the leader is available to assist in interpretation

and provide background information and to give leadership and guidance in the interaction of the group, the focus is on the group member and his participation so that he can discover vital truth for himself.

The leader frequently learns as much as does the group. He undergoes a type of in-service training, in the course of which he learns new skills in facilitating the development of the group and helping the members to achieve their potential.

3. *The Technique Utilizes Many Group Dynamic Principles.* This method of Bible study utilizes many of the principles of group dynamics. It tries to encourage group members to understand the interpersonal relationships of life.

Unfortunately, many of the ideas of group interaction have been confused by some of the extreme types of group processes known by such names as sensitivity training. Reading about the excesses of such groups, the Christian begins to have questions about any method using group dynamics.

We must constantly remind ourselves that many techniques of group dynamics stem from the Bible. The excesses that have marked many of the group experiences should not keep us from using good biblical techniques.

4. *Experiential Bible Study Is a Sharing Experience.* Experiential Bible Study is a sharing experience. Participants share their experiences with one another. This may become a practical demonstration of *koinonia,* the rich Greek word which literally means "going shares." Many sharing groups in church bring unusual blessing, but after a few sessions they begin to bog down. Experiential Bible Study guides the participants into a number of different areas around which sharing experiences can take place.

5. *This Type of Bible Study Calls for Action.* The group member not only sees the relationship of biblical principles to everyday life, but also must do something.

The type of Bible study recommended here can never replace diligent exegetical study of the Scriptures, but it will emphasize the personal factor, group involvement, sharing, and action, and will help the participant to realize that when it comes to the problem areas of life the Bible is as up to date as today's newspaper.

The Format of the Individual Programs

Because Experiential Bible Study is different from other types of Bible study, the programs are set out in a distinctive manner that is aimed at achieving the purpose of individual application, sharing, formulating principles, and initiating action projects.

You cannot read these programs to your group; neither can you memorize them and parrot them off. As the passage of Scripture itself is aimed at motivating action, so the materials presented here are stimulators to give the leader some ideas that will make the session more meaningful.

Each program is presented under a series of headings which occupy a special part in the total process.

Scripture

The reference from the Scripture provides the basis for the sessions. Although group dynamics enter into this experience, it is still Bible-based, and this passage of Scripture will give the clue as to what it is all about.

Psychodynamics

A psychological principle is supplied for each session. This material about the dynamics of individual experience, the way in which interpersonal relationships function, is provided to help the leader know what to look for in the interaction of the group. This material is not for presentation to the group but primarily for the leader's own information, so that he will understand what is happening within his group.

Handle this material carefully. Don't use it to build the idea that you are a psychologist who makes himself obnoxious by indicating he knows everything there is to know about the human psyche and spends his waking moments analyzing the way other people tick.

Remember, you are *not* a psychologist. You are a group leader who helps people, and you don't need to use psychological jargon.

Background

Because the whole emphasis is on the Bible, the leader must be familiar with the historical setting and the meaning of the Bible passage. Material in this section is mainly background material providing information to make the passage meaningful.

Once again, this material is not for presentation to the group in session, but it is to help the leader to be more knowledgeable in case Bible-centered discussion should eventuate later.

Sometimes a group member, puffed up with his own knowledge, condescendingly asks an embarrassing question that will test the leader's knowledge. It is hoped that the material here may be of assistance to the leader, at least provide a modicum of Bible knowledge that will help him put the biblical passage into its correct perspective.

Bible Reading

The passage suggested for the leader immediately raises the question of what version of the Scriptures will be used in the session. There was a time when it could be assumed that most people in church would be carrying—if they were Bible carriers—a King James Version. The situation has changed drastically in these days.

The multiplicity of versions has proliferated at an amazing rate, with first one version moving into the spotlight, then another. So you are faced with the test of versatility and deciding what to do about it. In the following chapters some suggestions will be made as to ways to overcome this problem.

One word of caution. Notice the objective of the session. Some versions may give the passage a different slant and not get across the idea, so read them carefully.

The Reflection Period

The technique used here is similar to that utilized in many

psychological tests that seek to reveal the inner life of the individual. The inkblot test is a good example. The subject is shown an inkblot and then invited to tell what he sees. It is really remarkable to listen to the testee pouring out reams of material about his inner life, with it all triggered by something that he saw in the inkblot.

In another type of projective test the individual is shown a picture of a scene and asked to tell what went before, what is happening at the moment, and what will be the outcome. Once again, many individuals pour out long stories of life experiences.

In Experiential Bible Study the whole situation is enhanced by using a biblical incident or passage. Many of these are familiar, and more than a few members of the class will already have a wealth of associations that can be utilized.

Sharing Our Associations

Here is the heart of the experience. You are involved in helping your group members have an experience of openness. Remind yourself of the importance of what you are doing.

When a person violates his value system, the natural, self-defeating reaction is to become secretive and closed off from one's fellows.

In the early church the Christians prized the experience by which an individual found his way back into fellowship; and the New Testament exhorts believers to "confess your faults one to another," and reports that the people who responded to the gospel message came, "confessing their sins."

Become aware of the importance of this part of the program from the perspective of both mental health and Christian experience.

The Emerging Principle of Interpersonal Relationships

In this segment the group tries to reach a conclusion about the principle or principles that are operative in situations such as this.

These principles must be expressed, as much as possible, in behavioral terms: What actions bring on what consequences?

My Action Commitment

This is an action program which centers on behavior. The members of the group are concentrating on their individual behavior. After identifying with the behavior in this Scripture passage, the participant moves toward observing his own personal behavior that was generally unsatisfactory.

Now the time has come for the group member to *do* something. Here is his opportunity.

STOP!

Go back and read this chapter again before moving any further. You must become familiar with the plan so that you can use the idea effectively.

When you have finished your second reading, move to the next chapter which contains a detailed description of the steps of the program.

4
Running a Successful Group

Experiential Bible Study places the leader in a different role from that which he occupies in a customary Bible study group. A leader in a regular group has to spend time studying the biblical text and trying to make sure that he understands it; then he has to work at devising ways of presenting his material to the class members. The leader of an Experiential Bible Study group also has to work on biblical text; but then a difference emerges. Instead of being a presenter of the material he is, by way of contrast, a facilitator who guides his group so that it does the real work.

This means the leader's role in Experiential Bible Study is much simpler and less demanding than it is in other types of study.

Right?

Wrong.

Although Experiential Bible Study is a comparatively simple technique of Bible study, it nevertheless requires work, in many instances, more work than does an usual type of Bible study. In addition to having a knowledge of the biblical text, the leader must be a student of personality and preeminently adept at the utilization of the principles of group dynamics.

To help you in the process of developing a leader's skills, we have provided a special feature, periodically spaced through the programs, called the "Leader's Workshop." These features highlight the techniques that have been used with other groups and found successful.

Despite all this there are distinctive methods that must be used in conducting an Experiential Bible Study period. You must start with preparation and then move into the steps of conducting the session.

Preparing for the Session

Most teachers in academic settings theorize that their students will spend two hours of personal study for each hour they are in class. In Experiential Bible Study you also must spend a minimum of this amount of time in preparation for your forty-minute class period. You will probably require more time than this, particularly in the beginning stages.

Your preparation should move through three steps.

Step 1. Note the *Scripture* reference. Read carefully through the passage prescribed for the session. You should give it at least three readings so that you become very familiar with it.

Step 2. Look at the *Psychodynamics.* Study the material dealing with the psychological principles that may emerge in the group so that you will be ready for them and know what you're looking for. A grasp of this body of material will probably help you in deciding what your emphasis should be.

Step 3. Review the *Background.* This material provides information about the Bible passage. You should study the Scripture in one or more of the modern versions as well as the King James Version. You could also profit by consulting a commentary.

Study time is never wasted. It sometimes seems disproportionate, but the more time you spend in preparing, the better you will feel as you go to meet your group. It will help to give you a feeling of confidence and will probably affect the way in which you go about your presentation.

Conducting the Session

How punctual are you? Because the leader's example counts so much with·this method, you should make sure to get to your meeting place on time, or even better, ahead of time. You can calmly welcome your group members as they come and help to establish a good atmosphere for your group.

Step 1. Check out the arrangement of the chairs. Avoid like the plague any arrangement that makes the participants feel they are spectators. Place the chairs in a circle so that each member can see all the others.

Step 2. As the group members arrive, greet them warmly and confidently. Try to make sure they are all introduced to each other. When you move into the group explain what is happening. You might say, "This is a different way of studying the Bible, which we call Experiential Bible Study. We are trying to apply the teachings of the Bible to the problems of everyday life. As we read the Scriptures, concentrate on trying to see the parallels between the Scripture episode and things that happen to you. I know you will enjoy this involvement experience."

Step 3. Read the Scripture passage. There are different ways of doing this:

> The leader reads.
>
> The group reads in unison.
>
> The members of the group read a verse in succession.
>
> The verses are read alternatively, the leader first, then the group.
>
> The men and women read alternatively.
>
> A gifted reader reads the passage to the group.
>
> One reader reads from the King James Version and another reader from a modern translation, such as *The Living Bible*.

Pay particular attention to this reading process, as it is a very important part in your experience as a group.

Step 4. Lead the group in the *Reflection Period*. Make sure you emphasize the importance of each person's individual associations as he or she sits and thinks about the passage. You might mention something about its being like looking at pictures in the fire or some other process where you really let your imagination go. During this time you might also have some background music that would help in meditation.

Step 5. This is *the* vital segment of the experience as members are led to the *Sharing Our Associations* period. Notice particularly some of the problems you will encounter here:

Make a lot of every member of the group being "on task." Explain to them that being "on task" means paying close attention to whoever is speaking. Point out to the group that the way in which the members of the group listen may determine the contribution of the participant.

Warn about subgrouping. Some insecure group members seek to subgroup. This generally takes the form of whispering or making remarks that can be heard by people close by. Stop this quickly for it will destroy the interaction of your group.

You must model. A good leader gives a practical demonstration of the way the members of the group should function. If you're not quite sure about this, read the Leader's Workshop entitled "Modeling." Think over some past experience and lead off by telling about something that has happened to you.

As you seat the class members, try to make sure you position a good participant alongside you. With this seating arrangement you can be sure to be off to a good start. Try to place the shy people so they will have a chance to see a number of other people in action before their time comes.

Maintain a positive attitude. Don't let anyone say, "I'll pass." Make a statement such as, "We want everybody to participate. Our motto is 'No spectators, only participators.'"

Tell them, "The more you participate, the more you get out of it. The shyest person has something to say which will be of great value in making a contribution to the group."

If someone is having obvious difficulty, just say, "We'll leave you for the time being and come back later." Make sure that you give the impression that they are not going to be left out, and convey the idea to the group that everyone is going to participate.

Remember that by maintaining this positive attitude you can help the members of your group. They are going to have a wonderful experience, and you'll be the means of helping them have it.

Step 6. Lead the group naturally into the period in which they discuss *The Emerging Principle of Interpersonal Relationships.* Some of them may have difficulty at this point. Once again it is important for you to prepare yourself beforehand and try to see some of the principles which would evolve. Then you can model.

Make a statement. There are statements provided in the programs themselves so that you can see the way to go about it. Try to make this a group experience in which the group members come to a consensus.

Step 7. Focus on the emphasis of *My Action Commitment.* In this portion of the program you are trying to help each member of the group to decide what to do in the light of the experience which he has had in class today.

One way of doing this may be to have a Class Commitment Book. At the top of the page write, "My Commitment for the Week Commencing Sunday, March 14." During the Action Commitment Period, each member can write down a commitment for the coming week.

If you use this method, don't forget to check back on the following week as to whether or not the group member kept his or her assignment.

Go ahead now and use the programs. You're in for an exciting and rewarding experience in which you are going to help many people come to a new appreciation of the Bible.

PART II
The Programs of Experiential Bible Study

leader's workshop

Modeling

From reading the introductory material of this volume you might get the idea that the leader is not important in this type of group experience. This is not true. The leader is doubly important, particularly because of the factor of "modeling" in teaching a group. *Imitative learning* is one of the hottest ideas in the field of education today.

• A marriage counselor who wants his clients to learn to relate to each other in more meaningful ways sits down and demonstrates the way it should be done: the expert says the counselor is "modeling."

• A leader working with a group of drug addicts tells them his story of how he was once hooked on dope and now has the habit under control. Sociologist Yablonsky notes the leader has become a "role model,"—an example of what the addict may be able to accomplish through the program he is about to enter upon.

• An Integrity Therapist sits down with a troubled person and, after listening to the troubled one's story, tells about an experience in life where he entered upon a period of depression. He is now able to look back and see the way his irresponsible behavior brought on his malaise, and he asks, "Does my experience have any relationship to yours?" He is using the technique which they call "modeling the role."

• A psychologist working on a toilet-training project hands the child a shaggy, Thirsty Baby doll and lets him give it a drink of water. When the doll simulates urination, the psychologist helps the child give the doll a potato chip and comments that the reason for giving the chip was that the doll had behaved "like a big girl." The child sees the doll rewarded for its good behavior.

Modeling, role model, modeling the role—all refer to the techniques by which one person demonstrates to another some new way of behaving.

In each of these programs the leader is going to have to learn to model, and also to train the members of the group so that they too can model before other group members.

1
Alone

Scripture: Luke 19:1-10

Psychodynamics

Life is lived in a constant web of relationships. Some psychologists tell us we cannot understand our personalities apart from experiences of interaction with other people. So Harry Stack Sullivan says that personality is "the relatively enduring pattern of recurrent interpersonal situations which characterize a human life."

When an inmate of a prison misbehaves and is given maximum punishment, that punishment generally takes the form of solitary confinement. To be separated from our fellows is the supreme penalty. Strangely enough, people often inflict punishment upon themselves, as they have a tendency to pull away from their fellows and deny themselves this most important experience of relationship.

Remind yourself of the enterprise upon which you have embarked in Experiential Bible Study. Your work in helping people, some of whom are lonely and alienated from their fellows, may result in their finding their way back into experiences of relationship and affiliation.

Background

You could commence by talking about the position that Zacchaeus occupied in the society of his day. The Romans had conquered Israel and were taxing the Jewish people. To collect the taxes, the Romans sold the privileges to Jewish individuals who were then able to add a percentage for themselves. These tax gatherers, or publicans, as they are called in the King James

Version, were not popular with the people.

Most of the Jewish people considered a Jew working as a tax collector for the oppressive enemy a traitor to his own race. Consequently, though a tax gatherer might be wealthy, he often lived a lonely life isolated from his fellow Jews.

The Sharing Session

The Physical Setting

How are your people grouped? The very worst way is to have them sitting in rows. If they sit like this, they are expecting to be entertained or to watch a presentation before them without any participation in it. Have your group sit in a circle. Make sure there are no vacant seats or spaces. Insist that all the chairs be as close together as possible.

The Bible Reading

Introduce the Bible reading by saying, "This is a different type of Bible study called Experiential Bible Study. So while we are reading you should take particular notice of what the passage is saying." Suggest to the group that they read around the circle, each one reading a single verse.

The Reflection Period

Ask the class to reflect on the passage which has been read. Then ask that they spend some time in quietness, just sitting, contemplating that story.

Sharing Our Associations

Remind the group once again that the associations they have are uniquely theirs. Ask them what associations come to their mind when they think of this passage.

Say to the group, "We are now going to share our associations. Remember that we want everybody to participate." There is often a very timid person who thinks he can't, but wait silently with an encouraging smile and allow him time.

"Let me lead off. When I think of the Zacchaeus story, I remember an experience which I think parallels the attitude people had towards this tax gatherer.

"I was driving up the highway from Beaumont, Texas, in my new car. As I came through one of the small towns south of Fort Worth, I saw a small store where they were selling gasoline very cheaply, so I decided to buy some.

"The man who came out to fill my car was a Latin American and was smoking a big cigar. In my mind there came a picture of my car blowing up, and so I said, 'Would you mind not smoking that cigar while you're putting gas into my tank?'

"He looked at me and responded, 'I do it all the time.'

"I replied, 'I'd rather you didn't do it while filling my car.'

"He reacted, 'If I can't smoke, I can't sell you any gas.'

"I put the cap back on the gas tank and drove off.

"I was furious, and within myself I said, 'That's these Mexicans. They're careless.'

"Of course I was wrong. The man just happened to be a Mexican, but he could have easily been a U.S. citizen or an Australian, for that matter."

You should then turn toward the first person in the group. "Well, Joe, why don't you share *your* associations with us?"

The Emerging Principle of Interpersonal Relationships

Lead the group to formulate a principle of interpersonal relationships which emerges from this Zacchaeus experience. It might be:

"We should not judge a person by his work or nationality."

"People who seem nicely fixed with material things are often lonely people."

My Action Commitment

Some of the following could be offered:

"I am going to go up to one lonely looking person this week and introduce myself."

"I have resolved to contact the church and find a shut-in that I can call on."

2
Imitative Learning

Scripture: John 13:1-17; 1 Peter 2:21

Psychodynamics

One of the newest ways of teaching is also one of the oldest known to mankind. It is sometimes referred to as imitative learning or "modeling the role," a process whereby the teacher demonstrates by example the lesson that is to be taught.

When exhibitors tried to import the movie *Skyjack* into Australia, Donald Chip, at that time the Customs and Excise Minister, refused permission and explained his action by saying, "The film deals with the hijacking of a crowded passenger plane by a mentally disturbed U.S. Army sergeant. The method of hijacking and of holding a crew and passengers hostage are explicitly and vividly depicted. . . . The experiences of airlines and civil aviation authorities have shown that the hijacking techniques employed in films are reproduced in real life a short time later."

By his action Chip was showing that he believed in imitative learning, as it is employed in education today.

Today's program focuses on the process of imitative learning or role modeling.

The Sharing Session

The Physical Setting

Do you have trouble getting started? Try to get your group in on time. Nothing is worse than being interrupted by latecomers. Urge the group to be punctual; leave chairs in a convenient place so that individuals can get in without interrupting the rest of the group once you are underway.

Background

William Barclay, the noted Scottish Bible interpreter, says that Paul's ethic is an ethic of *imitation* and notes the number of times Paul uses the idea of imitation. Of course, the idea is not peculiar to Paul. It is used frequently in the New Testament.

Christians are told to be imitators of God (Eph. 5:1); they are also exhorted to imitate Christ (Eph. 4:20; 1 Pet. 2:21); and the great personalities of the Christian faith are to be imitated by Christians: "Consider the outcome of their life and imitate their faith" (Heb. 13:7).

Paul also uses the idea of modeling in reference to his teaching ministry and frequently tells the Christians to imitate him: "I urge you to be imitators of me" (1 Cor. 4:14); "Be imitators of me as I am of Christ" (1 Cor. 11:1).

It becomes very obvious that the New Testament has anticipated many of the ideas of modern educational procedures and has a lot to say about what one authority calls "imitative learning."

Bible Reading

Do you like modern translations? Some of them are very good. However, in reading around the group it may become a little confusing if one has a King James Version, the next one, *Good News for Modern Man*, and the next *The Living Bible*. One good idea might be to have two people read, one from the King James Version, and the other, the same verse from a modern translation. It might not only give variety, but also throw some light on the meaning of the passage.

The Reflection Period

Suggest to your group members that they spend a period of time reflecting on these passages of Scripture. Remind them again about the importance of their personal associations.

Sharing Our Associations .

You can see by the nature of this program just how important it is that the leader set an example before the group. If the leader does not enter into the experience wholeheartedly and become frank and open about his or her own experience, it is highly improbable that the rest of the members will be very frank in their responses.

If I were conducting the group on this program I would say, "This passage reminds me of an experience I had some years ago.

"I used to set a rabbit trap in the bottom of a brickpit. The only way down to the floor of the pit was by a precipitous pathway leading down the side.

"Each afternoon I would pick up my small son, put him on my shoulder, walk across the field, and climb down the pathway to the brickpit bottom.

"One afternoon it was raining, so I decided to go without my son. When I got to the pit, I found the pathway wet and slippery. I gingerly climbed down the hazardous pathway. When I was about halfway down, I stopped and held onto a branch projecting from the wall of the pit. I began to wonder if I were not foolish to have come.

"As I stood there, a stone came rolling by, and I looked up to see my little son tottering down the treacherous pathway.

"I spoke quickly to him: 'Warwick, don't come any farther. Stand there, son.'

"I climbed up to him, picked him up in my arms, and began the difficult climb to the top of the pit. Though it was a bitterly cold day, by the time I arrived at the top the perspiration was pouring out of me, and a voice seemed to say, 'That's the way it is. Where you go, he goes. Where you plant your feet, he places his.' "

After you have modeled, turn and invite the class members to express their associations.

The Emerging Principle of Interpersonal Relationships

Ask the group to help you formulate a principle of interpersonal relationships. Some of their ideas might be these:

"I can see that my actions affect other people."

"If imitative learning has any validity, my children will learn more from what I do than from what I say."

"As a Christian I need to set an example before people."

My Action Commitment

Margo Kitterman gives us an example of the way in which she makes an action commitment. She says, "I have been fussing at my children about not keeping their rooms tidy. It has finally dawned on me that I have been untidy myself. I have resolved that next week I'll work on my own untidy habits; then I'll demonstrate to the kids just how I can keep my room tidy and then ask them to work on theirs."

3
Excuses, Excuses, Excuses

Scripture: Luke 14:16-24

Psychodynamics

If you don't want to do something, you can always find an excuse. And it doesn't matter how unreasonable or illogical the action, you can provide a logical reason for it. Psychologists call this process "rationalization."

Rationalization is sometimes referred to as the "counterfeit of reason." It is a mental activity by which, once we desire something strongly enough, we formulate a rationale for whatever we propose to do.

Background

Be careful with this program. It focuses on a parable told by Jesus. The parable spoke about the way in which people refused to respond to the gospel invitation, and many in your group will probably want to talk about the theological implications of the passage. But avoid theological discussion at all costs.

You could spend some time pointing out just how ludicrous were the reasons offered by people for not turning up at the banquet to which they had already accepted invitations. One had purchased a piece of land without ever having seen it. One had bought beasts of burden, unseen, and never tried them. A newly married man was refusing an opportunity to eat out.

You may want to point out to your group members just how transparently weak are many of the excuses that we offer as we evade our responsibility.

The Sharing Session

The Physical Setting

Ever tried having your group meet in a home? Remember the way in which the early Christians gathered in their "house churches." In this type of meeting you may be able to involve your neighbors or other people you could not normally reach.

There are some hazards—crying children, interruption of tradesmen, problems of seating, enthusiastic hostesses who may insist on elaborate refreshments. Despite all this, home Bible study groups have tremendous potential.

Bible Reading

Luke 14:16-24 is a well-known passage, and this might be a good time to have a reading in unison. It would also be an excellent opportunity to have the reading in succession, because of the way that the message carries through the passage.

Reflection Period

Suggest that the group think about excuses, and the way in which we personally and individually offer excuses to avoid things that might not work or that might be a trifle unpleasant. Suggest that as we sit together we flood our minds with some of the experiences that normally we might not be willing to discuss. Call on each person to be really completely honest.

Sharing Our Associations

Making an admission of using excuses to cover up for irresponsible behavior isn't easy, so the leader's modeling will be very important.

Thomas White is leading his group and says, "I have always had a problem in getting up and starting into the day. So when I landed a job with the Union Insurance Company, I realized I'd have to watch myself.

"I discovered my boss was an eager beaver. I don't know whether he suffers from insomina or not, but he was at work every morning at 7:30, and he made it clear that I must be on the job by 8:00 A.M. so that the operation would be in top gear by the end of the day.

"Well, I had trouble from the beginning. I just couldn't get up and get going. Whenever I arrived late, there was the boss, looking over the top of his glasses at me.

"Then my wife and I went to the annual class reunion and we didn't get in till 1:00 A.M. After arriving home, I watched the late movie. My wife suggested that I set the alarm; however, I replied that I could wake up—but I overslept.

"The boss came around later in the day and gave me quite a session, indicating my lateness had bugged him and I'd better do better.

"Two months later came an opportunity for promotion, and they gave the position to Ed Wiggens. I told my wife the reason Ed got the job was that he and the boss were both Aggies and were palsy-walsy.

"But I know now it wasn't any college affiliation. It was my lateness, and I'm just going to have to do something about it."

The Emerging Principle of Interpersonal Relationships

Help your group to establish some generalized principles. Here are some examples:

"I fool myself if I think I can fool other people by offering excuses for all my failures."

"If I keep on making excuses for every mistake, I'll never learn."

"I must be willing to face my own problems."

My Action Commitment

Talk to your group again about the importance of action. There's no sense in discussing our failures, wallowing in our misery, and refusing to do something about it.

These commitments are some they might make:

"I am going to commit myself to a program of self-improvement by realistically facing my actions."

"When I make a mistake, I am going to admit it."

"I will take as my maxim, 'A man is never stronger than when he's admitting his weaknesses.'"

4
Learning to Love

Scripture: 1 Corinthians 13

Psychodynamics

Recall the three Greek words for love: *Eros,* the selfish, emotional, romantic; *philia,* the companionate, intellectual; and *agape,* the giving love.

Agape is the rich word of the New Testament, the distinctive Christian word; the essence of it is the idea of giving.

In his ministry Jesus said, "A new commandment I give unto you, that you love one another." What was new about this? In the Old Testament the Hebrews were told to "love one another." The distinctive was "as I have loved you."

Jesus set the example by his willingness to give himself, which reached its ultimate in his death on the cross.

Background

The Epistle to the Corinthians seems to be an unlikely spot in which to discover the celebrated "learn to love." Most of the epistle is given over to a discussion of a number of controversies.

Paul is writing at white heat and taking his readers to task for immoral and disorderly conduct and is resolutely maintaining his apostolic authority in defiance of all the challenges of dissident groups in the Corinthian church.

In the midst of all this, Paul turns to the subject of giving love. He urges his readers to follow "a more excellent way."

The Sharing Session

The Bible Reading

The thirteenth chapter of First Corinthians is so beautiful and well known that you might be able to do something special. You could have some special background music on the love theme.

The Reflection Period

Tell the group, "This is a familiar passage and there is a good chance it will have memories for you. We will allow thirty seconds of silence while we consider this passage."

Sharing Our Associations

A good way to come at this would be to emphasize the giving quality of agape love. You could say, "Today you are able to give your experience to others. As we share our associations, you will be giving something to the group, perhaps a very intangible something, but, nevertheless, you will be giving it."

Betty Russel leads off with her group. "When I read the verse 'Rejoiceth not in iniquity,' I remember there is one translation that says, 'Love is never glad when others go wrong.'

"I remember how much I competed with Jean Simpson. We went through school together, graduated the same day. But she beat me. She married Marion Detrich, a highly successful architect, and when they moved into their $90,000 home, I couldn't help thinking of what a cracker box of a house I had to live in.

"Jim and I have done pretty well but never made it up to Jeannie's standard, and, whenever I meet her, she sarcastically asks, 'Where are you living these days, Betty?'

"Then the scandal over the new Power House broke open, and as a result Marion Detrich has gone into bankruptcy. My natural impulse is to be elated over Jeannie's misfortune, but I can see, in light of this passage, that would be wrong. I'm going to offer my friendship in a way I've never done before."

The Emerging Principle of Interpersonal Relationships

Help the group now to formulate a principle of interpersonal relationships. These might be suggested:

"Love is more than just an emotional reaction. I must *do* something."

"Love demands that I go into action and demonstrate how I feel."

"If I am truly Christian, I'll remember that Jesus' love took him to the cross. My love will lead me to do something for my fellowman."

My Action Commitment

Recall the group to the fact that this is agape love, a love which does something. In the light of what we have talked about today, there is some action that we need to take.

Betty Russel might model by saying, "I personally am going to get in touch with my friend who has been through such a bad experience, and I'm going to be just as kind and as generous as I can."

leader's workshop

Principles of Self-Help Groups

Within my book *Farewell to the Lonely Crowd* I endeavored to find out what it was that made the self-help groups so effective. I finally discovered some series of principles that were involved:

Socialization. There are no wallflowers in self-help groups. Newcomers are thrust into contact with other people. There is a constant round of meetings, classes, and conferences, and the newcomer learns he need never be lonely again.

Responsibility. Self-help groups insist that every individual must accept responsibility for himself. He is not allowed to blame others even for such desperate problems as obesity, drug addiction, alcoholism.

High Standards. In contradistinction to many of the modern schemes of therapy so permissive in their attitudes towards their patients, the self-helpers set high standards for their members and make heavy demands upon them.

Slogans and Epigrams. Most of these self-helpers have developed slogans or epigrams which enable them to remember some important facet of their program. Alcoholics Anonymous uses such ones as "Easy does it," "A day at a time," "Think, think, think."

Lay Leadership. Self-help groups may be a revolt against professionalism and an affirmation of the value of the common man. Lay leadership is probably the most noteworthy and universally seen single feature of the self-helpers. It is their common denominator.

Confession. All the self-help groups have some form of confession. They have discovered that men are alike in no one factor so much as in moral failure, and that he who confesses has dropped his pretenses and declared himself at one with the failures of the world.

Activity. Life is one long rush in a self-help group. When Alcoholics Anonymous says, "Take it easy," they don't mean sit still, for they are going to run the alcoholic off his feet. In some groups life is one constant hectic round of meetings, classes, and conferences.

Modeling. In the self-help groups the leader is meant to be a model. When he stands before his fellows, he talks about his own failures and presents before them an image of what they can do.

Failure in Success. Rather unfortunately, self-help groups, which start so wonderfully well, have the tendency to mature, to become wealthy and affluent, or to develop organizations, and all too frequently when this happens, they fail.

5

Maturing

Scripture: Luke 7:31-35; 1 Corinthians 13:11

Psychodynamics

Our program for today centers on the subject of maturity. The word "mature" simply means to grow, and the maturing person must be aware that life is a continual process of growth and development. A maturing person will have a number of characteristics.

The maturing person is a *creature of emotions but not their slave.* Emotional reactions are essential for survival, but they are primitive responses. We must beware of reacting at an earlier emotional level and grow emotionally as well as physically and intellectually.

The maturing person is *guided by long-term purposes* rather than immediate desires. A popular definition of maturity is "the capacity to postpone pleasure," and it contains a great deal of truth. Allport says it in another way: "Every mature personality may be said to travel towards a port of destination, selected in advance, on to several ports in succession."

The maturing person has a *perspective on life beyond his own self-interest.* All of life is a socializing process during which we learn the futility of self-centeredness. A person with no sense of involvement with other people will always remain immature.

The maturing person develops a *capacity for self-objectivication.* Socrates asserted, "I must first know myself," and, unfortunately, self-knowledge doesn't come easily. We must cultivate the ability to take an inventory periodically of our strengths and weaknesses.

The maturing person has a *unifying philosophy of life*. The really mature person has some focal point around which the processes of the personality are gathered. Obviously our individual faith in Christ is of primary importance here.

The continually developing maturing process is hindered by two mechanisms; fixation, which means holding or stopping, or regressing, which refers to a process of retreating to an earlier level of development.

Background

Children love dressing up and playing games—apparently it was always this way.

In Jesus' day there were two favorite games, funerals and weddings; and, of all places, the children liked to play their games in the busy marketplace.

Weddings was a game in which two of the children dressed as bride and groom; ahead of them went the piper playing his happy tune, while a great group of kiddies skipped joyfully behind the wedding procession.

Strangely enough, funerals was also a popular game. Several of the children carried a makeshift coffin on their shoulders while a group of the others, wearing sackcloth and marked with ashes, cried and mourned with a remarkable imitation of the way in which their parents behaved at funerals. The point of Jesus' story in Luke 7 was that some of the children sat at the side of the marketplace. They refused to play weddings because they thought the game was too flippant. On the other hand, they would not play funerals because it was too sad. Our Lord said people refused to respond to the teaching of John the Baptist because he was too stern, and to the message of Jesus because it was too happy. In other words, they were unresponsive.

But we are going to focus on Jesus' words in which he said that people were like children. Couple with this the statement of Paul, "When I was a child, I spoke as a child, I understood as a child, . . . but when I became a man, I put away childish things."

We must be continually maturing people.

The Sharing Session

Bible Reading

Since the passages are short, ask two people to read them first from the King James Version and then from a modern version.

Reflection Period

Follow the reading with the reflection period. Remind the class members about the uniqueness of their individual associations. Ask them to prepare to share these associations.

Sharing Our Associations

Today we will look over the shoulder of Oscar Scarborough as he leads his group. Oscar says, "As I was reflecting on these passages, I thought of many times when I have behaved in a childish way. One incident stands out with startling vividness."

Oscar pauses. "I hate to admit this, but I actually changed Christmas. It happened this way. I have two children, and I decided that, as I like working in my workshop, I would make all their Christmas presents for this particular year.

"My wife, Susan, was taken with the idea at first, but, as Christmas drew nearer and I was obviously not getting the toys made, she became more apprehensive. She suggested that maybe she should go ahead and buy some toys, but I was adamant. I would make them. Then I had to work overtime.

"Well, we came right up to Christmas and still the toys were not finished, so I insisted we have a family conference, and I announced that Christmas would be two weeks late. In our home January 8 would be Christmas Day.

"We had the most miserable Christmas. I worked in the basement, Susan tried to keep the kids busy, and a spirit of gloom fell over our house. Looking back over it, I see what a childish attitude I had."

Oscar turns to a group member and says, "Well, Jim, would you care to share your associations with us?"

The Emerging Principle of Interpersonal Relationships

Give the group a chance now to verbalize their ideas about what might be the principle of interpersonal relationships that comes from this instance. They might suggest:

"I have come to see that when I am completely self-centered and do not think about other people, I am being very immature."

"Children are generally unwilling to admit they have made a mistake. When I take an adamant position like this, I am being childish."

"One popular definition of maturity is the capacity to postpone pleasure. I can see how my willingness to deny myself will help me be more effective in helping others, and I'll be better myself."

My Action Commitment

"I've been after my husband to buy a new car. Deep down I realize that we should really wait, and I'm going to tell him to hold up until we get into a better financial position."

"I've come to see that I am too preoccupied with my own little world, and I'm going to be involved with helping someone else."

6
Sibling Rivalry

Scripture: Genesis 37:3-11

Psychodynamics

Students of human growth and development have long noted the interplay of relationships between the various members of the family. Some have emphasized the importance of birth order, claiming that the first child may be the favored one, or the second child is forever trying to overtake the first, being determined to upset the accepted order of things, while the last child is frequently thought of as being the favored one and consequently spoiled.

Some authorities in the field have noted the peculiar relationship of children and parents, so Freud spoke about the Oedipus complex in which a peculiar relationship came to exist between the boy and his mother, with the father seen as a rival and, from the other perspective, the little girl moving towards her father and seeing her mother as being the threatening one. The interplay of relationships within the family situation is seen particularly clearly in today's Experiential Bible Study Program.

Background

Review some of the events leading up to this situation. Jacob, the father, watching his sons and the discord developing amongst them, must have found his mind going back to his own boyhood days. He had been his mother's favorite, and she had pushed him into deceiving his father so that he could receive the paternal blessing rather than the older brother, Esau. He finally had to flee from home to avoid his brother's wrath.

While living with his Uncle Laban, he had been the victim

of a deception himself. Jacob's uncle had promised him that in payment for seven year's work he would be given the hand of his beloved Rachel; but, when the time came, Laban insisted that Jacob should marry the older Leah and work for seven more years before he could finally take Rachel for his wife.

Jacob ultimately became the father of twelve sons and these, in turn, founded the twelve tribes of Israel.

After Jacob underwent a profound spiritual experience, Jehovah changed Jacob's name to Israel and promised to make a great nation of his progeny.

Joseph was one of the two sons of Jacob's beloved Rachel and the son of his old age, and by virtue of these facts had a special place in Jacob's affection. As we read the story of Joseph, he appears as a very virtuous young man, but at times, a little priggish, and it is easy to see how he could be irritating to his brothers.

The Sharing Session

The Physical Setting

Do you ever noticed the way in which people form themselves into cliques? Try to discourage this. Ask the members of the group to sit next to different people each time they come so they can get to know other members of the group. Try to think out ways to keep them all mixed up so they will not develop a habit of sitting with particular groups of people.

Bible Reading

You might like to have the whole group read the Bible passage in unison.

The Reflection Period

Tell the group that we are going to think about this passage of Scripture. It has a family theme and probably stirs up memories of relationships we may have had at some time or another within our own family group. Remind them again, "Your associations are your own personal property. They are distinctively yours. Think for a few moments about this passage and how it applies to your own personal situation."

Sharing Our Associations

Larry Rupert introduces the situation by telling about an experience of his own. He says, "I grew up in a good-size family, but not as large as the one to which Joseph belonged. I was the oldest child, and I was never as bright as the others. I had a sister who bugged me. She was bright and vivacious and always brought home good grades from school.

"Whenever we had guests she used to be paraded as the bright one, and I always had the feeling that I was the dummy. When we would go somewhere, I would often feel a little shy, but she would push in. I hated it when people would say, 'Oh, you're Jeanie's brother.'

"When Jeanie went to college she had some problems adjusting and dropped out. I remember how secretly delighted I was. However, with passing years I've come to see that each individual has his own gifts, and I don't have to be concerned about my sister. In later years Jeanie has sometimes bugged me, but really she's a good old girl.

"Now remember, your associations are your own personal possession. Let's hear what associations you have in your mind."

Then go around the circle and give them each an opportunity to speak about their associations.

The Emerging Principle of Interpersonal Relationships

What principle seems to surface here? There are a number of possibilities.

"When I am envious of someone else's abilities, it hurts me more than him."

"If I hold hostility in my heart, it may lead to my taking some foolish action."

My Action Commitment

Larry says, "I'm going to make a special trip to visit Jeanie and tell her about how unfair I have been in my attitude toward her."

7
Handling Depression

Scripture: 1 Kings 19:1-13

Psychodynamics

"Life, liberty, and the pursuit of happiness." A pretty fruitless pursuit it is for some people. Although happiness is such a highly desirable experience, the closest many people get to it is an experience of the opposite—depression. For the depressed person life looks black, "like inky clouds rolling up over me," one sufferer described it.

One way of expressing this is to say the basic formula of depression is

$$D = S + P$$

In this formulation, depression equals sadness plus pessimism. The pessimism component is all important. Many experiences in life can cause sadness, but in depression the subject feels life is hopeless, there is no way out of it.

Some aspects of depression:

While some crisis may trigger it, the reaction is out of all proportion to the precipitating factor.

Lowered self-worth, a feeling of valuelessness.

Slowing down of activity. No desire to move, just to sit still and do nothing.

A pattern of withdrawing from other people.

A feeling of helplessness. As one subject put it, "I felt as if forces outside of me were controlling me."

It has long been noted that depression may be a form of unconscious self-punishment. Because of this, some forms of therapy emphasize the importance of the individual's taking some radical actions in handling the reaction.

Background

The Elijah of chapter 19 of First Kings is altogether different from the Elijah of chapter 18. In chapter 18 he is the triumphant prophet confronting the hordes of the prophets of Baal and emerging triumphant. Now he is fearful of a woman, a woman of no mean stature, to be sure, for Jezebel had a deserved reputation of power and strength.

Elijah fled and took refuge under the juniper tree. Notice that this was actually a tiny shrub, "a variety of broom which is one of the most characteristic shrubs of the deserts of Southern Palestine and southward to Egypt. Though the shade it affords is but scanty, in the absence of other shrubs it is frequently used by desert travelers as a refuge from the sun's scorching rays (cf 1 Kings 19:4). The root yields good charcoal, giving out much heat (Ps. 120:4)."

Notice Elijah's pattern of withdrawal.

Verse   3. He arose and went for his life.
Verse   4. He went a day's journey into the wilderness and came and sat down under the broom tree.
Verse   4. Elijah said, "Oh, Lord take away my life."
Verse   9. He came hither into a cave.
Verse 10. Only I am left.

Look also at the completely unrealistic view Elijah had of his situation. "I only am left." But God reminds him, "Yet I have left seven thousand in Israel who have not bowed the knee to Baal."

Notice also the way in which God manifests himself as seen in verses 11 and 12. During the course of the discussion you might raise the point as to how people really know God and know when God is speaking to them. You might be able to talk about an individual's conscience and the indwelling Holy Spirit. This might be a good starting point for a discussion of such subjects as the way in which God speaks today.

The Sharing Session

The Physical Setting

Remind your group of the importance of being "on task," that is, paying attention to all that is happening. If someone is whispering or reading or in some way failing to pay attention to the preceding, suggest, "Let's all make sure we're on task."

The Bible Reading

The passage for reading is 1 Kings 19:1-15. Why not try reading the passage alternately? The leader can read the first verse and the group the second and so on.

Reflection Period

Invite the group to reflect on the passage just read. You might say, "Most of us have had spells of depression at some time or another. We will probably have very little difficulty in identifying what is going on in this passage." Give the group thirty seconds to think about it.

Sharing Our Associations

Remind the group about the distinctiveness of their associations. No one has the same associations as another. Commence by modeling. Recall some experience in which you were depressed.

Marvin Jackson, a successful writer, is leading his group: "Early in my writing career I had worked for a long time on a book that I felt should make a good seller. A salesman from a publisher had urged me to submit the manuscript to his publishing company rather than to the one I had in mind.

"After having sent the manuscript off, I waited anxiously to get a reply. When it finally came, I was in Florida, staying in a beach house. I drove into town to the post office to pick up the mail, and there was the letter I had looked for for so long.

"The publisher told me he didn't think he could publish the book. Worst of all, he enclosed an evaluation by an anonymous psychologist, which was very critical of my work.

"After I read that critical report, my spirits plunged. It was like a slap in the face. When I got back to the house, I felt I didn't want my wife to see that letter; so instead of going in, I walked around the house and made my way down to the beach and went for a long miserable walk. As I walked I wallowed in my misery, and my depression deepened. I had a terrible morning.

"The original publisher later produced the book, so I had spent an unnecessary morning of misery."

Marvin turns to the next man in the circle, "Why don't you share your associations?"

The Emerging Principle of Interpersonal Relationships

Ask the group what they think is the principle of interpersonal relationships that we find in this incident. Some of their suggestions might be:

"When I'm depressed I need other people."

"I must learn to move towards rather than away from people."

"Although I feel like lying down and resting when I'm depressed, I need to get up and get going."

My Action Commitment

Try something a little different today. Point out the way that God dealt with this depressed prophet. In chapter 16 there are a series of strong commands for action.

Verse 9.   What doest thou here, Elijah?

Verse 11. Go forth and stand on the mount.

Verse 13. What doest thou here, Elijah?

Verse 15. Go, return.

This gives us a clue for some of the action commitments that we might make. Marvin Jackson says, "In this coming week I am going to prepare myself, and when my depression comes I am moving into action."

8

The Inner Struggle

Scripture: Romans 7:15-25

Psychodynamics

Life's decisions always involve conflicts, especially when they have to do with values. Personality theorists have had a busy time trying to come up with ways of explaining what is going on in the decision-making process when a moral choice is made.

One way of doing this is to speak about systems of personality. In this method the primitive part of personality is called the "id," the values which an individual holds are referred to as the "superego," and the mediating, decision-making self is sometimes called the "ego."

Most moral decisions are made in consideration of the id forces, which represent many factors that would bring pleasure at any given time, and the superego, the system that is constantly reminding us "you ought" and "thou shalt not."

Some psychologists see the id forces as having to do with sex and aggression, and these are the two drives that give most of us a lot of problems in the business of living.

Background

Paul's Epistle to the Romans is a profoundly theological document in which the inspired writer puts down in writing many of the great doctrines of the Christian faith.

Two themes are constantly raised in the course of the letter, the sinfulness of man and the holiness of God. As these are discussed, Paul clarifies the part played by the atoning death of Christ in bridging the gap between God and man.

The equivalent of this conflict between good and evil is seen by Paul as he looks into his own personality and views what he calls his old nature and his new nature. Paul realizes that the way of victory is through Christ, but he feels completely frustrated because he fails so often, and he cries out, "O wretched man that I am."

The Sharing Session

Bible Reading

As you look around the group, you might tell them you are about to lead them now in the Bible reading portion of the experience. It might be a good idea to fill them in on a little bit of the background as to what is going on here and how frustrated the apostle Paul feels. Decide on what method of reading you will use this time. Reading around the circle is obviously one good way to do it.

The Reflection Period

Invite the group to spend a short period of time reflecting on the passage. Let us ask ourselves what it really means, particularly, what it means to us individually and personally.

Sharing Our Associations

Invite the group to share their own personal associations. George Brewster is leading his group.

"As I read about Paul and the struggle he had within himself, I was reminded of an experience I had last year when I bought our new car. I really worked on that deal and enjoyed haggling with the salesman. I've always been interested in the way car salesmen figure their prices, and, as he worked on his figures, I kept an eagle eye on him.

"As he figured, I was on top of him, and I noticed a mistake in addition. Of course, he didn't ask me to check it; in fact he seemed to be working hard at trying to prevent my seeing what he was doing.

"When he gave me the final figures, I knew, from the other bids I'd gotten on the same car, that he had made a mistake of $500—in my favor.

"I told him I'd take the car, and we settled the deal. That night when I got home I swung between elation and concern. I told myself it didn't make any difference; those dealers gip people all the time.

"The next day at work I got a call from the sales manager. He told me the salesman had made a mistake in figuring the price of the car. He said the rule was that the sales manager must always okay the salesman's price, but he was away at the hospital, and the salesman had gone ahead without his approval. He said there was nothing he could do about it legally but he was appealing to me.

"I took a tough stand and said that I knew my rights and I had no intention of paying any more.

"When I told by buddy, Harry Jones, he was tickled. He said it was the first time he'd ever heard of a customer gipping a car salesman.

"For a week I struggled with myself, but at last I went down and paid the extra $500."

The Emerging Principle of Interpersonal Relationships

This is not an easy session to handle in formulating a principle of interpersonal relationships, as it mainly has to do with the internal struggles of personality. A typical formulation might be: "I realize that my personal inner struggles generally affect other people, and I need to make good decisions."

My Action Commitment

A good action commitment might be, "I've decided I'm going to identify with my best impulses when I make my decisions."

Leader's workshop

Alcoholics Anonymous Twelve Steps

The grandfather of the helping groups is Alcoholics Anonymous. Basic to all their work are their famous Twelve Steps. Study them, and you will find some ideas to help with your groups.

1. We admitted we were powerless over alcohol, . . . that our lives had become unmanageable.
2. We came to believe that a Power greater than ourselves could restore us to sanity.
3. We made a decision to turn our will and our lives over to the care of God *as we understood him.*
4. We made a searching and fearless moral inventory of ourselves.
5. We admitted to God, to ourselves, and to another human being the exact nature of our wrongs.
6. We were entirely ready to have God remove all these defects of character.
7. We humbly asked him to remove our shortcomings.
8. We made a list of all persons we had harmed and became willing to make amends to them all.
9. We made direct amends to such people wherever possible, except when to do so would injure them or others.
10. We continued to take personal inventory and when we were wrong promptly admitted it.
11. We sought through prayer and meditation to improve our conscious contact with God *as we understood him,* praying only for knowledge of his will for us and the power to carry that out.
12. Having had a spiritual awakening as the result of these Steps, we tried to carry this message to alcoholics, and to practice these principles in all our affairs.

9
Restitution

Scripture: Leviticus 6:1-5; Numbers 5:6-7; Luke 19:8

Psychodynamics

Workers in the helping profession have discovered restitution! The discovery has helped to give rise to the notion of psychoeconomics.

The word guilt has a significant root. Originally it was the payment of a fine for an offense. It comes to us from the Anglo-Saxon word "gylt," meaning to pay. At a conference on Integrity Therapy, a rabbi pointed out that in Yiddish the world "gelt" means money. Of guilt, Tournier says: "It is inscribed on the human heart: everything must be paid for." McKenzie asserts: "Guilt must be paid for."

This may mean that guilty people will have to make payments, not to gain forgiveness, but to feel better within themselves.

Alcoholics Anonymous has stated the situation very clearly in steps 8 and 9 of their famous Twelve Steps: (8) Made a list of all persons we had harmed and became willing to make amends to them all; and (9) Made direct amends to such people wherever possible except when to do so would injure them or others.

In today's program we are going to examine the subject of restitution and the need that many of us have for this experience.

Background

Our Bible passages for today have many lessons, but we are focusing on the subject of restitution, which is clearly defined in the Old Testament.

The code of King Hammurabi decreed: "If a man has struck his father, his hand shall be cut off. If a man has caused the loss of a patrician's limb, he shall shatter his limb. If a man has made the tooth of a man who is his equal to fall out, one shall make his tooth fall out." This principle is found among many of the primitive peoples: the thief loses a hand, the adulterer may be castrated, the perjurer has his tongue removed. One authority quotes the instance of a man who killed another by falling on him from a tree. The penalty was that a relative of the deceased was to climb a tree and fall upon the murderer and so enact justice.

The Old Testament has a similar theme: "Whoso sheddeth man's blood, by man shall his blood be shed"; or, "Thou shalt give life for life, eye for eye, tooth for tooth, hand for hand, foot for foot, burning for burning, wound for wound, stripe for stripe" (Ex. 21:23-25). Later came the principle of restitution. In the theft of an ox, the restitution was to be fivefold; a sheep, fourfold; and in property damage, the simple equivalent was all that was necessary. Other instances were covered by the command that tells the transgressor to repay and add one fifth to it.

The Zacchaeus incident shows the way one man made restitution. After his experience of salvation, Zacchaeus wanted to return the money he had stolen from people. He wasn't content merely to add the one fifth that the law demanded but decided to restore fourfold what he had taken. But he also realized there were many people to whom he had not made restitution, so he gave half his goods to feed the poor.

Here is a beautiful illustration of catching the spirit of restitution.

The Sharing Session

The Physical Setting

Try to keep a good mix of your group. Watch particularly any sort of discussion that goes on within the group. Don't have people forming themselves into little subgroups. It might be a good idea to stay on the alert, and when you see a couple of people whispering to each other, to say, "Don't forget, no sub-grouping."

Bible Reading

Is there someone in your group who has specialized in dramatic or other types of readings? Why not ask this person to do the reading while the others sit and listen.

Reflection Period

Try some music today. If you could get a recording of a hymn such as "Jesus Paid It All," it might create a good contemplative atmosphere. You could say to your group, "Did you ever look at pictures in the fire? It is a great experience. You sit in front of the fire on a winter's evening, and you look at the dancing flames. It won't be long before you see all sorts of images. Of course, This is similar to the experience you may have today as you consider these passages on restitution. Let your imagination run riot as you think about the statements contained in these passages."

Sharing Our Associations

Recall to your group the distinctive setting in which we are functioning, the way in which we are sharing experiences, and the way my associations might help you, and yours may assist me.

Commence by setting the example. Francine Butler, leading her group, says: "When I was a student in university, I went through a period of depression. I often wondered why I should be feeling so depressed and concluded to my own satisfaction that my problem was that I was working too hard. The hours that I was spending in the library and at my job were combining to pull me down.

"Then I began to ask myself if there was anything wrong in my life. And I knew there was.

"I felt my professor had given me too many assignments. One was due soon and I didn't have it ready. I had noted that the professor was somewhat careless in the way in which he gathered up the materials, and I saw there was plenty of room for mistakes.

"When he handed back the assignments, I put on a bold face, went up, and asked where mine was. He looked over his book and said he had no record of it's being turned in. I stoutly maintained that I had turned in my work and I couldn't understand what could have happened to it. The professor was bluffed by what I said. He acknowledged that sometimes papers went astray; and so he gave me an "A" for the paper that I never turned in.

"As I went through my period of depression, I realized the time had come for me to do something about my relationship with this professor. I went to him and told him what I had done.

"He looked at me and said, 'What do you think you should do?'

"I replied that I was willing to do whatever he would suggest, and I realized that I really should make some restitution. In line with this I would be willing to write a paper for him.

"The professor agreed to this line of action. I wrote a paper and turned it in, and almost immediately I began to feel better."

After you have finished modelling turn to the next member of the group and say, "Do you have something you would like to share with us?"

The Emerging Principle of Interpersonal Relationships

Ask your group what principle of interpersonal relationships they find emerging from our discussion today. Some characteristic answers might be:

"Although I know God forgives my sin without my doing anything about it, if I am to feel good, I must put things right.

"When I make confession, I need to take it all another step and to do something about putting things right."

"Even when I cannot repay the person that I may have hurt, I can feel better myself if I help other people."

My Action Commitment

We are all going to make an action commitment today. You might lead off. "I am going to make a review of my behavior, and, where I've pulled a blooper, I'm going to do something about it—not just say I'm sorry, but undertake to *do* something.

10
The Anxiety Problem

Scripture: Matthew 6:24-34

Psychodynamics

In many ways man's capacity to experience reactions of fear is one of his greatest assets. Because he experiences fear, he will look both ways before crossing the road, take care of his body, and make provision for his family.

Unfortunately, some aspects of fear can tie us up in knots and prevent us from realizing our true potential. One of these is the experience we call anxiety.

Anxiety differs from fear in that a person who experiences fear sees some direct and clear object, such as a fierce dog, and realizes the danger. By way of contrast, anxiety is the vague sense of uneasiness that there is some threat of indefinite forces from without or within our own personalities.

The same situation is true of man's capacity to anticipate. This is good and helps him to plan ahead, but if he is forever worrying about the future, he can become frustrated and overanxious.

The experience of anxiety is so widespread that some authorities believe it to be the root of all other neurotic reactions.

We should remember that the antithesis of fear is faith—a certainty that God is for us and nothing will happen to us without him.

Background

You may need to spend some time in explaining the command in the King James Version, "take no thought." Explain that it means "be not overanxious." In *The Living Bible* it is translated "Don't worry." Obviously, this does not mean that we should not look ahead or make plans for the future. It is simply telling us not to be overanxious.

Note that in this passage there are three sections, each of which is introduced by the statement "Take no thought."

1. Anxious thought is contrary to the lessons of nature, which show it to be unnecessary. (Matt. 6:25-30.)
2. Anxious thought is contrary to the lessons of revelation, which show it to be heathenism. (Matt. 6:31-32.)
3. Anxious thought is contrary to the scheme of providence, which shows it to be unnecessary. (Matt. 6:33.)

This is a passage of Scripture that may tempt you to dissipate your time in expounding and doing some preaching. Resist this inclination and help the members of the group to associate with the passage.

The Sharing Session

The Bible Reading

This passage is beautifully rendered in the King James Version, but *The Living Bible* makes its meaning clearer. Try having one reader use the King James and another to follow with each verse as it is paraphrased in *The Living Bible.*

The Reflection Period

You might say, "Our passage for this morning has presented us with one of the great problems of humanity—facing anxiety. Let's spend thirty seconds thinking about this situation and about what the Bible suggests for us."

Sharing Our Associations

Elizabeth O'Neil is leading her group and commences by modeling.

"I suppose you could say I'm a worrywart. Jim—that's my husband—always says I anticipate the worst, and then, no matter how badly things come out, I'm ready for it.

"My father died shortly after I was born, and I guess my mother had a bad time trying to raise us. She was never quite sure where the next meal was coming from, and I suppose she communicated some of this anxiety to me, for, as I have entered into married life, I've had a tendency to have this same attitude.

"I worry about my husband, my children, my church, the state of the economy, world peace—anything, you name it—I worry about it.

"But as I associate with this passage today, I have a feeling that all this is a negation of my faith. I'm going to try to leave it all in the hands of God and let him do the worrying."

The Emerging Principle of Interpersonal Relationships

Lead the group in formulating some principles, some of which might be

"Today is the tomorrow I worried about yesterday, and it never happened."

"When I worry, I show a lack of faith, in God and in my fellowman."

My Action Commitment

Elizabeth O'Neil sets the example by making her commitment: "I have decided I'm not going to be a worrywart any longer. I'm going to learn several verses such as "Casting all your care on him for he careth for you"; "I can do all things through Christ who strengtheneth me."

"The moment an anxious thought comes into my mind, I'm going to repeat these verses and endeavor to vanquish it and to replace anxiety with faith."

11
Husband-Wife Relationships

Scripture: Ephesians 5:21-33

Psychodynamics

Psychologists are at last catching up with the Bible. One of the newest ideas of psychologists is called behavior modifiers and involves the setting up of contracts between husbands and wives.

A husband and wife who undertake this line of action decide to face realistically their relationship and to locate the points of friction that might be causing conflicts in their marriage.

Each partner lists the three behaviors of the spouse which are most undesirable; and then they set about trading off behaviors with each other. They start with the least undesirable and enter into an agreement. One such agreement might read.

Pat and Harry Nevin's Behavioral Exchange Contract #1

Harry agrees that he will be home promptly each evening by 6:30 P.M. for supper or call early enough for Pat to change supper plans, and Pat agrees to be up each morning and have Harry's breakfast prepared by 7:15 A.M. _____

_____

After they had worked on this behavior for a week, they decided on a more significant problem area.

Such an agreement is referred to as a Behavioral Exchange Agreement. Each spouse is willing to exchange a behavior.

Background

You might want to compare this passage from Ephesians with similar ones in Colossians 3:18-21 and 1 Peter 3:1-8. In each of these passages is to be found the ethic of reciprocity. In Ephesians Paul speaks of three areas of reciprocal relationship.

Servants are urged to be obedient to their masters and to serve them honestly, while the masters are told to behave well toward the servants, remembering that they themselves are the servants of Christ (6:5-9).

Parent-child relationships interact. The children are reminded that the commandment "Honor thy father and thy mother" is the first commandment which has a promise implied with it. But fathers are reminded that they must be understanding with their children and not make unreasonable demands that will annoy and frustrate them (6:1-4).

At the peak of these relationships stands that of the husband and wife, which is also to be on a reciprocal basis. Our passage for today's focus begins with "Submitting yourselves *one to another* in the fear of the Lord," and then admonishes the wife to submit herself unto her husband. Then it moves on to a word about the husband's attitude toward his wife, "Husbands, love your wives, even as Christ also loved the church, and gave himself for it." In many ways, it is easier for the wife to submit herself unto her husband than it is for the husband to love his wife as Christ loved the church.

The all-important note is reciprocity. Both husband and wife must play their respective roles as they interact with each other.

The Sharing Session

The Bible Reading

Try an alternative reading with men reading the first verse and women the second verse through the passage.

The Reflection Period

The passage today is hitting at the most fundamental relationships of life, those of servants and masters, parents and children, husbands and wives. Let us reflect on these relationships and what they mean to us.

Sharing Our Associations

As an illustration of the way in which a leader might conduct the session, let us look in on Katie May Kelley.

Katie May says, "It is particularly appropriate that we should read this passage alternatively today because it has a series of associations about the reciprocity of the relationships of male and female.

"As I sat here thinking during the reflection period, my mind went back to the struggle I've had in deciding my role in marriage.

"I don't really have any aspirations to be an out-and-out Women's Libber," she smiles. "I've never really considered burning my bra, but I've often felt how unfair many things in life are, as far as women are concerned. And, after listening to Sanya Hansen, who lives down the street, I began to wonder if our churches were not male strongholds. The pastor is a man, and so are all the deacons; yet it is the women who provide the bulk of the work force.

"It also irritated me when some preacher held forth on the importance of women submitting themselves unto their husbands.

"One day, Don, that's my husband, began to tease me. I guess I was foolish to take him seriously, but he quoted that passage from First Peter and reminded me that wives should be subject to their own husbands, 'even as Sara obeyed Abraham, calling him lord.'

"I turned and glared at him. 'You're not my lord.'

"Well, we finally got it worked out and sat down for a sensible discussion about our roles in marriage. I came to see that it's much easier for me to submit myself to Don than for Don to love me, as Christ loved the church."

The Emerging Principle of Interpersonal Relationships

Motivate the group to work on principles of reciprocity within family life. Some of these might be as follows:

"I've come to realize the best way to *get* things in the family is to be willing to *give*."

"A husband and wife relationship is never a one-way street. What I do affects my husband, and what my husband does affects me."

My Action Commitment

One of the men in the group might say, "I've been telling myself how good I am to my wife, and I've failed to see that the most important thing I can give her is my love. I've decided to spend more of my time giving her the love and attention that I know she needs."

12
Pouting

Scripture: 1 Kings 21:1-7

Psychodynamics

No single experience of human beings highlights the importance of interpersonal relationships as clearly as the reaction that is generally referred to as "pouting" or "sulking."

Pouting is a nonverbal means of communication in which a person sinks into silence, a hostile, belligerent silence, which tells the person with whom he has a difference that, like some medieval lord, he is building an emotional wall and refusing to speak to the person he is trying to punish.

The pouting person turns in on himself. Sulking is frequently used to describe this reaction. A sulky is a two-wheeled, horse-drawn vehicle that has room for only one person. When a person sulks, he isolates himself from his fellows and lives in lonely separation.

Preeminently, sulking is a technique of attacking another person. We lack the courage to come right out and attack the individual, and so we do it by withdrawing from him.

Background

Pouting, or sulking, was part of the ongoing conflict between the prophet Elijah and King Ahab.

Ahab was a wealthy man but also a tyrant. Whenever he looked out from his window and saw the vineyard of Naboth, he could not help thinking how nice it would look as an herb garden. So he offered to purchase the land. But Naboth saw the situation differently. The land had come to him as an inheritance and he did not want to part with it.

Peeved by Naboth's refusal, Ahab behaved like a petulant child, and, throwing himself upon his bed, turned his face to the wall and refused to eat.

Ahab's attitude inevitably attracted the attention of his aggressive wife, Jezebel. It seems possible that, knowing her nature and capacity for getting things done, Ahab wanted her to take over and manage the situation. Jezebel went into action. She devised a plan whereby she had Naboth killed and the land became Ahab's.

The Sharing Session

The Bible Reading

You may have some difficulty today in deciding how much of the passage to read, but verses 1-7 would seem to be a good choice.

Commence by saying, "We are moving into a new phase of our Experiential Bible Study today. Let's not get caught up too much in the extraneous material. We are focusing on attitudes. Let us note Ahab particularly.

Reflection Period

Follow the procedure of having your class reflect on the passage you have just read. Remind them of the uniqueness of their associations. No two persons in the class have the same associations, and all the class is anxious to hear them.

Sharing Our Associations

Let us look at the way Ronald Pringle modeled before his group. "When I read about Ahab lying on his bed, turning his head away and refusing to eat, it brings home to me a painful memory of my own attitude towards life and the way in which I have pouted to try to get my way.

"I once worked for a company where I had a good relationship with Mr. Harrison, my supervisor. I liked my work, and he often told me how much he appreciated my conscientious application to my job and all that I was doing to help the company.

"Then came the word that someone was going to be sent to London, England. Our company had just bought out a business there and now planned to send a couple of office people who knew the routines to work there, in order to teach the English employees the way we wanted things done.

"It caused quite a buzz around the office, and we all agreed how highly desirable this position was. It was whispered around that Mr. Harrison would be making the recommendations. I felt sure that he would mention me. Imagine my chagrin when I learned that Jim Seft and Alex Sarafen had been selected for the London positions.

"Well, I was disappointed—and mad at Jim Harrison. After all that line he'd been giving me about how valuable I was to him and to the company, and now when this opportunity came he had passed me up. I knew I could hardly say anything to him so I decided I just wouldn't talk to him. I completely cut him off. Whenever he came by and wanted to discuss something, I was curt and got away as quickly as I could. Gradually, a great gulf came between us. I misinterpreted everything he did. Whenever something went wrong and I seemed to come out on the wrong end, I felt he was trying to get at me. When he tried to explain, I just turned away.

"For four whole months I wallowed in my misery, and then the manager called me in. He told me that word had come to him about my strained relationship with my supervisor. He said that it was creating a very bad situation in the office. Then he added, 'The unfortunate part about all this is that Mr. Harrison is planning on leaving us at the end of the year to go into business with his brother, and he has recommended you as his successor. That's the reason you were not sent to the London office. The problem now is that, with all this tension in the office, there is grave doubt as to whether you would really be the one to take Mr. Harrison's position. I am sorry about it.'

"By my sulking I'd failed to get the true facts and had entirely misconstrued the whole situation."

Ronald Pringle now turned and invited the other members of the group to share their associations.

The Emerging Principle of Interpersonal Relationships

Encourage the group to work on formulating a principle of interpersonal relationships as it emerges from the discussion of the experiences of pouting. Some of these might be their suggestions:

"Sulking brings me a satisfaction, but it hurts others."

"Sulking is infantile. An adult must develop more mature ways of handling situations."

"Sulking is the worst type of negative communication."

My Action Commitment

When I feel like pouting I'll take several actions, such as (1) "I'll recall that pouting is a selfish reaction and will try to think of others"; or (2) "I will refuse to isolate myself and will take some positive actions to help someone else."

leader's workshop

Integrity Therapy Principles

Integrity Therapy is based on the importance of an individual's value system and takes an optimistic view of the role of conscience in personality. The basic principles are these:

1. Integrity Therapy rejects all deterministic theories which make man a victim of heredity or environment. Every individual is responsible for his own life, and exercises his right by making his own decisions.

2. Each individual has a conscience, or value system. When he violates his conscience, he becomes guilty, a condition which is not a sickness but a result of his wrongdoing and irresponsibility.

3. A common reaction to personal wrongdoing is to cover up and deny its existence. In this secrecy, guilt gives rise to symptoms which may be so severe as to upset life's balance.

4. As secrecy causes man trouble and separates him from his fellows, so openness with "significant others" is the road back to normality.

5. Openness takes place with increasing numbers of "significant others" and progresses in ever-widening circles as the individual learns to live authentically with his fellows.

6. By itself, however, openness is not enough. The guilty individual is under an obligation to make restitution appropriate to the acknowledged failure in his life.

7. The only way to become a whole person is not only to remain open and make restitution, but also to feel a responsibility to carry the "Good News" to others.

13
Friendship

Scripture: 2 Samuel 1:17-27

Psychodynamics

The word "love" is an umbrella term and may be best understood as involving three levels with Greek names: *eros,* selfish, romantic, emotional love; *philia,* companionate love; *agape,* gift love. In this session we are focusing on *philia,* the companionate love or friendship.

Friendship is quite different from *eros,* or romantic love. This may be seen in a number of contrasts between the two.

Romantic love is fostered by differences, and two people in the throes of an emotional love experience will ignore differences that may become particularly annoying when the infatuation subsides. Friendship, on the other hand, lacks the *eros* emotional and sexual reinforcement, but depends on an affinity of interests which cements and holds the friends together.

Friends and romantic lovers face in different directions. Romantic lovers are face to face, with the loved object absorbing all the lovers' attention. In contrast, friends are in an entirely different posture, side by side, looking in the same direction. They are bound together by their mutual interests.

Romantic lovers build a fanciful image of their beloved in which the beloved is idealized and the faults are overlooked. Friends, on the other hand, know only too well the shortcomings of each other, and there is no necessity to avoid these, for they are an integral part of a distinctive personality.

Possibly the most outstanding difference between romantic love and friendship is that eros love is between two people. They generally have the attitude of "How can we get away from these people and be by ourselves?" Friendship, on the other hand, can involve any number. In fact, the greater the number it involves, the more satisfactory it is likely to become. And jealousy, which has been seen as the nurse of romantic love, has no part in friendship. We are happy to share a friend and proud of the opportunities which come his way.

Background

The Israelites had a collection of martial songs kept in a book known as the book of Jasher (pronounced Yasher). One of the most moving of these songs, or odes, is the passage which we are studying today.

This particular ode is sometimes called a lamentation or a dirge. It has a certain military connotation and is referred to as the "Song of the Bow," the bow being the most frequently used military weapon of that day.

The dirge falls into two parts, with the first part including verses 19-24 and referring to both Saul and Jonathan, and the latter, verses 25-26, concentrating on Jonathan alone.

David and Jonathan were drawn to each other as young men. When they first met, it was written, "the soul of Jonathan was knit to the soul of David, and Jonathan loved him as his own soul. . . . Then Jonathan and David made a covenant, because he loved him as his own soul" (1 Sam. 18:1,3).

In the fluctuating relationships which David had with Jonathan's father Saul, Jonathan stood by his friend and warned David when he feared his mentally disturbed father might destroy his friend. In all their relationships, Jonathan always proved himself to be the highest example of a true friend.

The Sharing Session

The Bible Reading

Do you have some person who is a gifted reader? Ask him or her to read this beautiful passage of Scripture.

Reflection Period

Remind your group that although this is one of the most beautiful passages to be found in all literature, we want to look beyond the actual words to the experience of friendship, which may be a lost factor in human experience today. Call upon them again to associate themselves with the statements of the passage.

Sharing Our Associations

Don Wickman is leading his group, and in the process he models before calling upon the other members to respond.

"I suppose that all this stuff about homosexuality has caused many of us to become a little leery about friendship with someone of our own sex, but I often wonder if many of us are not missing out in friendship experiences.

"I suppose the first cloud over my friendship with Morris came when I began to get serious about Judy. I was forever arranging double dates, and, one night, Judy raised the question about my friendship with Morris. She said that if she married me—and she let me know that was an 'if'—she didn't want to share me with Morris.

"Well I was crazy about Judy, and I quickly made up my mind and began to see less and less of Morris.

"When Judy and I launched out in life, we settled in Kansas City. One day, quite by accident, I discovered that Morris—now married to Dawn and with two children of his own—was living about ten miles west of us.

"I really wanted to renew that friendship, but I worried about Judy. Finally I sat down and talked things over with her. You can imagine how pleasantly surprised I was to discover she no longer saw Morris as a threat. She has also become pals with Dawn, and we spend many happy hours together. Our friendship has been a very meaningful experience."

The Emerging Principle of Interpersonal Relationships

Assist the group to formulate some of the ideas about friendship that come out of the discussion, such as

"I can differ with someone and still enjoy his friendship."

"The New Testament idea of *koinonia*, or fellowship, is important in all of life."

My Action Commitment

"I am going to spend more time cultivating friendships and enjoying relationships with other people."

"I have decided never just to walk into church and out again without greeting someone else and making some friendly gesture."

14

Parent-Child Relationships

Scripture: 1 Samuel 1:19-28; Ephesians 6:1-4

Psychodynamics

A family unit should be a vibrant, growing, developing organism. It has its beginning when two people commit themselves to each other; it then passes through several stages: childbearing; having preschool children, school-age children, teenagers; and then launching the grown children into a life where they can repeat the cycle in their own experience.

Many married couples do not really begin to live until they have children of their own. Yet children bring peculiar problems. While children may provide a focal point for the love and interest of the couple, these same children may also bring peculiar strains upon the husband-wife relationship.

Although we have been through a permissive era in parent-child relationships in America, and now live in a society in which the notion of permissiveness is widely accepted, we will note that the Bible knows little of this idea.

The book of Proverbs is full of wisdom, "Train up a child in the way he should go" (Prov. 22:16). The verb refers to a soldier in the army being trained; so the parent has a responsibility for training the children. But it also means "dedicate," and so the parent must be dedicated to that task. Proverbs also states a positive position in discipline: "Don't hesitate to discipline a child. A good beating won't kill him. As a matter of fact, it may save his life" (Prov. 23:12, "Wisdom for Modern Man").

In the language of some modern psychologists, we need to discover who is manipulating whom. There is a pattern of interaction in family life which is to be understood, or else we may be replacing the old idea of parent domination with the new idea of child domination.

Background

Two passages of Scripture come under our consideration today. The first is from the book of Samuel and tells of the anguish of Hannah's heart. In the Hebrew society women were frequently judged by their ability to bear children, and "barren" was a word that cut like a lash.

Hannah went up to the temple and prayed that God would give her a child. The priest, Eli, seeing her in the temple, finally told her that God would grant her petition.

After the birth of her son, Hannah watched over him with care. When Samuel was three years old, she took him to the temple as an offering to the Lord, saying, "I have loaned him unto the Lord."

In the Ephesian passage we find that the note of reciprocity which characterized husband-wife relationships is also a factor in parent-child relationships. Children are to honor their parents and obey their parents, but parents are to be careful not to provoke their children to wrath.

The Sharing Session

The Bible Reading

As this is a family situation, it might be well to have a husband and wife read the passages in unison.

The Reflection Period

Because our lives are so bound up with our children, there are sure to be many associations stirred by these passages. Allow the usual thirty seconds for reflection.

Sharing Our Associations

Guide your group into the sharing session by calling their attention to the uniqueness of their associations.

Helen Boyd is leading her group. She says, "It is said that the birth of a child is the culminating point of a marriage, and I know that the arrival of our first child certainly gave our marriage a new focal point.

"As our family grew to three children, we found our lives revolving around our children. It sometimes seemed as if we had no life of our own.

"Someone has said that America used to be God's country, but now it's kid's country, and what we can do, the sort of food we eat, the time we have for ourselves are all determined by our children.

"I guess reading through these verses in Ephesians makes me realize I owe it to my children to insist that they grow up to be obedient and responsive to what Bill and I think they ought to do. On the other hand, I am going to try to be reasonable and not provoke them to wrath."

The Emerging Principle of Interpersonal Relationship

This period can be intensely practical. Try to get your group members to think about their relationships with their children. Some of the principles might be

"Parents are responsible *to* their children and not *for* them. If the children don't turn out the way they should have, it might not always be the parents' fault."

"Parents and children interact with each other. We should be very careful not to let our children manipulate us but to stay in control of the situation."

My Action Commitment

Some action commitments that might emerge:

"I realize that children are very important, and I am going to spend more time with mine."

"I just have a couple of grown children, but now that I realize how important they are, I am going to spend some time working in organizations like Sunday School with the children."

"I am going to spend much more time preparing myself for my role as a parent."

15
Anger

Scripture: Matthew 5:17-24

Psychodynamics

There are several theories as to what people should do when they are annoyed. One popular view that has been widely disseminated is that it is dangerous to "bottle up" our emotions; we should express them. This attitude has helped to give rise to many of the techniques used for helping people "express themselves" and has given rise to a lot of "expressive therapy."

However, many of our experiences with this practice have been far from satisfactory. Some people who "express themselves" find, that rather than draining off emotions, they often just get madder by the moment and, in the process, hurt other people.

A group working with ex-mental-hospital patients, called Recovery, Inc., claims that temper is the greatest single problem in life, and this judgment might well be true.

One way of controlling temper is to follow the technique of Recovery, Inc. Following this technique, a person who is annoyed should do something—work out in the gym, work in the yard, play golf, and so on—to relieve the tension.

Remember, anger can destroy us. Dr. John Hunter, the famous anatomist, who had a heart condition, used to say, "My life is in the hands of any fool who cares to annoy me." Hunter was obviously referring to the danger of anger in his response to a foolish comment that was made to him.

Background

In the Sermon on the Mount, Jesus was teaching his followers about a higher way of life which is superior to that demanded by the law of Moses. He told his followers that his intention was not to destroy the law but to fulfill it, to present a superior way by which they are to live.

The whole message of the Sermon on the Mount focuses on the so-called sins of the spirit, such as lust and anger, and zeroes in on a person's attitude. The simple premise is that one's attitude might be just as damaging as the action itself. In relating her story of years spent in a concentration camp, Corrie ten Boom tells about a cruel jailor. This man made life for her and her husband a misery. As she brooded over this individual's cruelty and considered her attitude, Corrie reached a conclusion. "Didn't he and I stand together before the all-seeing God, convicted of the same sin of murder?"

The Sharing Session

The Bible Reading

Do you have someone in your group who does readings? This beautiful passage would challenge such a person.

The Reflection Period

Today's topic is very personal. Many people are unwilling to acknowledge the difficulties they have with temper. Give them time to think about it.

Sharing Our Associations

As the leader, you must be prepared to model this one.

George Murrey, leading his group, says, "This passage surely got at me this morning. I hate to admit it, but I have a terrible time with my temper.

"In the past I've referred to my temper as 'righteous indignation,' and I often quote the verse 'Be angry and sin not,' but in my saner moments I know this is an excuse.

"I'll never forget one day when I'd gone off to a nearby town for a conference. On the way back, a man who was following me honked me over, and when we stopped, he told me the back wheel of my car was wobbling all over the place.

"I immediately knew that Tim, my son, who had used the car the day before I left, had messed it up.

"When I arrived home, I came in storming. I yelled at Tim, upset my wife, and had the whole household in an uproar.

"It was days before we settled down again. After it was all over, I realized that by popping off I'd hurt myself, my wife, and my family.

"I'm going to remember a verse out of Proverbs, 'A soft answer turneth away wrath, but grievous words stir up anger' (15:1)."

The Emerging Principle of Interpersonal Relationships

Help the group formulate some principles of relationships that indicate the danger of anger, such as these:

"When I get mad I hurt myself and others as well."

"Losing my temper at home means I hurt the people I love most."

"The loss of self-control may lead to my loss of influence on other people."

My Action Commitment

Lead off by saying, "In consideration of the dangers in losing my temper I am resolving to do something about my hair-trigger responses. Perhaps I'll count up to ten before answering anything that annoys. And, as much as lies within me, I'll try to remember how my outbursts of anger affect other people."

leader's workshop

Unwelcome Visitors

Psychiatric Sam: wants to diagnose every situation. He leads the group into the "paralysis of analysis."

Prosecuting Priscilla: attacks people with a whole series of questions. She's been reading too many "who-dunnits."

Self-Righteous Cyril: cannot think of any mistakes that he has ever made. Apparently everyone else in the world has failed, but he really wants to spend the time polishing up his halo.

Talkative Thomas: always has something to say about every subject under discussion. He knows a little bit about everything, and therefore feels that he has to constantly keep on talking.

Retiring Rose: modestly maintains that she doesn't want to waste the group's time and feels that they could move on to give someone else a chance to talk. This is only a coverup, because she does not really want to participate.

Helpful Harry: seeing that one group member is feeling the heat, especially in an area where he is vulnerable himself, he feels that he will help his comrade with such a statement as "We all do that, don't we?" Implicitly, he hopes the other man will come to his rescue later on, when he is facing a difficult situation.

Poor Pete: always feels sorry for himself.

Hopeless Hannah: has an insoluble problem. It doesn't matter what is suggested, she has either tried it or decided it won't work.

16
Church and Family Relationships

Scripture: 1 Timothy 3:1-13; 5:1,2

Psychodynamics

Men and women need each other. The skill of living is the skill of relationship, and even avant-garde people, who have rejected the idea of the traditional family, almost invariably become a part of some type of group that provides the experiences of closeness they need.

Many of the modern communes are examples of this idea. Rejecting traditional family patterns, they nevertheless form themselves into groups that go by the name of "The Hicks Family" or something similar. In these efforts we sometimes see the *family spirit* as defeating the *family unit.*

In this day and age, when people are more mobile and families more fragile, many individuals will be looking around for experiences of affiliation within family-like units.

Our program for today will be concerned about the church as a family and about the family functioning as a church.

Background

The pastoral epistles of 1 and 2 Timothy and Titus are full of ideas about family life. Paul was writing to Timothy as his son in the faith and warning him about the temptations and problems he would be facing in the days ahead.

As he wrote, Paul came up with the idea that the church and the family are kindred organizations and interrelate with each other. As he developed the idea, he pointed to the church principle as being very important in family life and the family principle as significant in church life.

In essence, the idea is that the church is to be like a family. Many of their relationships are similar. Also, the family is to be like a church, worshiping and witnessing to the world around about it.

The Sharing Session

The Bible Reading

This will be an excellent passage to have read by the men and women, reading responsively.

The Reflection Period

Background music should go well today. Here's a good hymn, "The Church's One Foundation." You could say, "This passage today has to do with the two most important institutions to which men and women belong—the family and the church. Let's try and focus in our minds on what this passage has to say about these two institutions."

Sharing Our Associations

David Long is leading a group and starts the discussion: "Many years ago I heard a preacher quote some Catholic writer, who said, 'You cannot have God for your father, unless you have the church for your mother.' It was a catchy little statement, but I was never quite sure what it meant. In fact I'm not sure I know now.

"For a long time I was quite taken with the idea that the church was hurting the family. I listened to Sandy Kenson sounding off, and he said there were so many meetings at church that a man never had enough time with his family.

"So we bought a boat and began to spend a lot of our time at the lake, and our churchgoing grew more and more sporadic.

"Then my second boy, David, began to run around with the wrong crowd. One night the police arrested one of his friends for drunken driving, and I imagined all sorts of things happening.

"We decided that for the good of our family we needed to

return to our church. I can now see that the church ministers to the family as no other institution can, and I am glad that I am back in church again."

The Emerging Principle of Interpersonal Relationships

Some of the principles might be these:

"The church and the family walk hand in hand and should strengthen each other."

"We should see our fellow church members as brothers and sisters in Christ and treat them accordingly."

"The church is really a family of families."

My Action Commitment

Some possible action commitments:

"I am going to be sensible in my church obligations and not accept too much; but what I do accept, I'm going to be faithful to."

"I'm going to do more about extending Christian concern into my family, having prayer, Bible reading, and Bible studies in my home,"

17
Resentment

Scripture: Luke 10:38-42

Psychodynamics

One of the most widely known and least understood mechanisms of reaction in the human personality we call *resentment*. The word comes from two Latin words which literally mean "to feel back."

The Seven Steppers, an organization founded by Bill Sands, certainly know what that means. Sands, son of a Californian judge, and an ex-convict himself, has majored on rehabilitating convicts by a series of group experiences in the pre- and post-release period of prison life.

Appropriately for convicts, the Seven Steppers program of action is stated in the form of an acrostic formed on the word Freedom. In many ways, the crux of the program of Seven Steppers is contained in the fifth step: "Deciding that our freedom is worth more than our resentments, we are using that Power to help us free ourselves from these resentments."

Resentment presents a major problem for the convict. Leaving prison with a chip on his shoulder, he is vulnerable, he overreacts, makes an impulsive move, gets into trouble with the law, and finishes up back in the penitentiary once again, having lost the freedom toward which he had looked for so long.

But it is not only convicts. Many people spend their lives feeling backwards, as they hold resentments in their hearts.

Background

Jesus had long maintained a friendship with Mary, Martha, and Lazarus and loved to visit their home. This passage in Luke tells us about one such visit. The two women were delighted to have their guest, and each responded rather characteristically.

Martha, the energetic housekeeper, did everything she could to make Jesus welcome and hastened to prepare the meal.

Mary, on the other hand, was the contemplative type. She took her position at the Savior's feet, so as to catch every word that fell from his lips.

The energetic Martha, hard at work, was irked by the sight of her sister not involved in the chores of the household. She petulantly demanded that Jesus send her sister to work.

Like so many of us, Martha was resentful, and Jesus rebuked her.

The Sharing Session

The Bible Reading

Because of the nature of this Scripture passage, two women, reading responsively, could present it well.

The Reflection Period

Here we are, back in a domestic situation. Remember your associations are unique. Let your mind dwell on the biblical incident for thirty seconds.

Sharing Our Associations

Nancy Cummings is leading her group in the Mary-Martha session and says, "To me Martha represents someone who is resentful. She sees Mary sitting at Jesus' feet and thinks of all the work she has to do. It doesn't seem at all fair to her.

"In my mind I associate this with the experience I had with Henry some years ago.

"Just before our second child was born, Henry's mother wanted him to go to their hometown and finalize a real estate deal. It seems that she had a good chance to sell, but it had to be done immediately.

"Naturally I didn't want him to go, but he said, 'Babies never come on time, tomorrow I'll be back.'

"Well, the baby did come on time, and there I was, in the hospital, with no husband.

"I just can't forget that horrible experience and every time something goes wrong in my relationship with him, my mind is flooded with the memory of that night."

The Emerging Principle of Interpersonal Relationships

Invite the group to work together in formulating a principle or principles like these examples:

"If I am resentful, I an feeling back instead of looking ahead."

"When I am resentful, I'm letting the past dominate the present."

"Resentful people are tied up by an emotion."

My Action Commitment

Let's try something different today.

1. Have some of these "Resentment Reducers" copied off and give one to each member.

2. Encourage the group members to focus on one person towards whom they feel a resentment, and fill in his name on the top of the card.

3. Think about this person and write down six good qualities about him in the space provided.

4. Tell them to carry the card in a pocket or purse and use it as follows:

   The moment a resentful thought comes to mind, remove the card and look at it.

   Concentrate on stop—say it—shout.

   Think of six good points about the person involved.

RESENTMENT REDUCER

PROBLEM _____

STOP

The moment the cue comes—go into ACTION
* Concentrate on *STOP*
*Say it out *LOUD*
*If convenient *SHOUT*

THINK

Six of resentee's good points:

1. _____

2. _____

3. _____

4. _____

5. _____

6. _____

18

The Portrait of a Wife

Scripture: Proverbs 31:10-31

Psychodynamics

In a day when Women's Lib has raised its strident voice against male chauvinism, a great number of women are in the midst of an identity crisis. Many a woman wonders if she is not imprisoned in the straitjacket of a male-dominated culture, and she may have a desire for experiences of self-actualization.

Such thoughts seldom entered the mind of a Jewish female. Jewish women in Bible times accepted the fact of male dominance and were content to be subordinate to the all-powerful head of the family. The Jewish mother, however, appears to have worked behind the scenes subtly to manipulate the situation to gain her own ends.

The situation recalls the old story of the woman who said, "My husband is the head of our house—I am the neck."

The passage of Scripture under discussion today is remarkable in its message on the virtue of a woman, and is unique in Jewish literature, which is mainly concerned with the superiority of the male.

Note particularly the statement at the beginning of the chapter that these proverbs came from King Lemuel. They contrast with the proverbs in the other portion of the book which, we are told, were repeated to Solomon by *his father.* This present collection, in the last chapter of the book, is said to have been told to King Lemuel by *his mother.*

Background

The passage for today is really a beautiful Hebrew poem of

twenty-two verses. Following the style of one form of Hebrew poetry, it is an acrostic on the Hebrew alphabet, with successive Hebrew letters beginning the first word of each verse.

The remarkable woman portrayed here has many outstanding virtues, but she is preeminently a woman of action.

Reading of this industrious woman recalls the story of another Jewish woman, named Dorcas, of whom it was said, "This woman was full of good works," and adding, "which she did."

The Sharing Session

The Bible Reading

Why not try a different way of doing the Bible reading for today. Because of the difference between the King James and modern versions, it might be a good idea to use two versions. Have one member read from the King James Version. After the reading of each verse, have another member read from one of the modern translations. This will enable the group to hear the beauty of the King James Version and also appreciate the clarity of the more modern translation.

The Reflection Period

Call the attention of the group to the careless way we listen to material being read. You might say, "In these days when we are being bombarded with audio and visual stimuli, and are afflicted with what some people call 'noise pollution,' many of us are learning not to listen. Let's have thirty seconds of silence in which to concentrate on this passage and what we might learn from it."

Sharing Our Associations

Remind your group about the uniqueness of their personal associations. You might also point out that there are many subjects under discussion in this passage, and there is a good chance that there will be a variety of reactions.

Let us look in on Ken Smiles at work with his group. He says,

"The woman spoken of in Proverbs certainly must have been tremendous. As I see her, she is a real estate broker, supervisor, seamstress, and porter—it seems as if there is nothing she could not do.

"I sometimes think about my wife, and realize that, in many ways, she is just as remarkable. She is the mother of my children, she is my companion, she helps me earn the living, and I am just about convinced that she is just as capable as this woman whom the Bible says was worth more than precious gems.

"But I think the phrase that caught me was the one from *The Living Bible* which tells about the attitude of the husband towards his wife. It says, 'He praises her with these words: There are many fine women in the world, but you are the best of them all.' I really know in my heart of hearts that women need plenty of praise—men do, for that matter—but I think women need it even more. Rather unfortunately, that's just the commodity that I am short of. Even though my wife works so diligently and does so much for me, I very seldom stop to thank her and to tell her how much I appreciate what she is doing for me. As I read this chapter, I feel convicted about the fact that I have spoken so little to her in commending her in what she does."

Ken turns to the next member in the group and asks if he would care to share his associations.

The Emerging Principle of Interpersonal Relationships

If yours is a mixed group, you may have to present principles from both a masculine and feminine point of view.

One might be, "We men must realize how much our wives need our praise and commendation."

Another, "Even though a woman may feel the culture has built-in attitudes towards her, she has the ways of really influencing the destiny of a household."

My Action Commitment

A couple of typical commitments:

"I'm going to spend a lot more time looking for things to praise in my spouse."

"As a wife I'm going to get in and do some of the things about the house that I have been leaving to my husband."

leaders workshop

The Way East Ridge Does It

East Ridge is a community open to people who want to practice an intense application of the principles of Alcoholics Anonymous. They conduct sessions referred to as Big Ten Meetings. The meetings are held under a series of rules which they say are "not open to debate." A selection of these follows.

1. *There are no observers.* Everyone agrees to participate and to tell the truth about himself, his past and present behavior, and past and present feelings. Major emphasis is on one's present behavior and status as a human being. There is, quite naturally, considerable reference to the past but only in preparation for the fuller revelation of what is true about oneself in the present. Keep in mind AA's Tenth Step, for which the meetings are named: *Continued to take personal inventory and when we were wrong promptly admitted it.*

2. *No red-crossing.* When a participant has been asked a difficult question, or is in a difficult situation, no one is to rush to his defense with an easy answer or reassurance. Everyone attending is assumed to be adult and able to deal with whatever challenge comes his way without the intervention of a defender or nurse. While someone else is running (that is, is the center of group attention, and has the floor for an extended period to tell the group about himself), we may get a "carom shot" in identification with him, and our red-crossing is then really a defense of ourselves.

3. *No trip-taking.* Extended, monotonous recountings of past events, behavior, or feelings in which there is no longer much emotional investment, even for the person, are trips—archaeological trips. Windy, intellectual discourses, nowhere near personal needs or concerns, are trips—head trips. All trips are out of order in a Big Ten. This is sometimes a judgment call. Leadership and strength in the Big Ten will point the way.

4. *No subgrouping.* Attention of everyone in the group is at all times to be focused on the person running. There are no circumstances that warrant verbal exchanges between two or three participants in one corner that distract others and deny full attention to the person running.

5. *No rat-packing.* Participants are not to gang up to challenge the authority of the group. Challenge the untruth of people, not the ground rules.

6. *Don't psychoanalyze.* Don't use clinical terms. Stay away from dreams and symbols. Don't theorize, intellectualize, hypothesize. Keep near the heart (gut) feelings and away from mere problemizing.

7. *No stealing.* When someone has started a good line of questioning, follow up. Don't interrupt with a new line you propose. Hold it until there is a logical opening for a new track. And when someone is running, don't interrupt and take over the run yourself. It's all right to interject a comment in support or criticism, but if the interjection goes on too long, it's stealing.

8. *No guile.* Don't act falsely, use tricks, or put a person on with some false or contrived statement to see how he will react. Stay strictly away from all "techniques" and from needling.

9. *No bones.* Don't throw out a false problem, a bone. If, for example, you choose to get the group involved with you in a discussion of your money difficulties (for you, a purely mechanical, intellectual problem) in order to keep them away from a discussion of some problem in your life you are mortally afraid they will find out about, you have thrown a bone and, more than likely, aborted the good of the Big Ten for you. Your emotions will tell you what is important, and it's what you are feeling strongly about yourself *now* that you should talk about in the Big Ten.

10. *Protect anonymity.* Since Big Tens are AA meetings observe the usual rule: Do not disclose the AA membership of anyone in the Big Ten to anyone not in the group.

11. *Protect confidentiality.* When you come to East Ridge for a Big Ten meeting, you meet and work closely with members of the East Ridge Community and others here especially for the Big Ten. When you leave, don't discuss what anyone else said in the meeting with anyone not part of the East Ridge Community or the Big Ten meeting you attended. You are free to say what your own "run" was about; protect yours.

19
Assessing Values

Scripture: Luke 18:18-25; 21:1-4

Psychodynamics

Life is a constant process of decision-making, and overshadowing every decision is the scale of values by which we make our judgments.

We have long known that a state of conflict creates anxiety in the individual's mind. Faced with alternatives, he cannot decide which is the most important of his options.

Because of the type of society within which we live, money is one of the criteria by which we make our judgments, and faced with a decision, a person will often ask himself, What is there in this for me?

Many people live on this basis and, like Esau of old, sell their birthright for a "mess of pottage."

Today's session will center on making decisions about what is the most valuable asset in life; and we will see something of what people prize most.

Background

This is one of the most moving incidents in the New Testament. The young ruler is vibrant and full of life and, obviously, anxious to be identified with the best. As he approaches Jesus and addresses him as a good man, he eagerly asks what he must do to go to heaven.

Jesus leads off by checking the young man: "Why callest thou me good?" Jesus seems to imply that the young man might have been making his judgment of other people by a very low set of standards.

Then after the young man has listed all his virtues, Jesus lays down his final ultimatum, "Sell all thou hast and give to the poor"—which the rich man was unwilling to accept.

Contrast this with the story of the widow's mite, about the widow who gave all she had.

The Bible Reading

The reading for today would lend itself to reading alternatively. Let the leader read the first verse, the class the second verse, and so on through the passage.

Reflection Period

Call the attention of the group to the message of the passage about values of life. Ask them to let their minds associate with what is happening in this passage, particularly as to what we count to be of the greatest value.

Sharing Our Associations

Peter Hammack is leading his group and says, "This isn't going to be easy for me because I'm afraid this story hits close to home.

"I grew up in a home where we always had to struggle for existence, and money did not come easily to us, with the result that in many ways I am a tightwad. I get to thinking about how difficult it is to earn money and what inflation is going to do to our bank account, and so I turn each penny on its edge and try to make our money go as far as I can.

"Of course I was never like this rich young ruler. I didn't have any great material resources, and becoming a Christian never involved my facing up to the challenge of what I'd do with my money.

"But as the years passed I became more and more absorbed in my business. My church attendance decreased, and I was attending only occasionally, but I kept telling myself my first duty was to provide the living for my family.

"One year the church was in a campaign for a new building.

They were soliciting contributions, and I took a strong stand against it. I not only refused to give, but also went around campaigning for other people to withhold their contributions.

"Then came a crisis in my financial affairs. I had a partner who was a real go-getter, but I suddenly discovered that he had been siphoning off a lot of our money, and we finished up in a bankruptcy procedure.

"In my desperation I began to pray about the hopeless situation that was developing, and I came to see that money had been my god. I've made up my mind that I'm going to keep my family and look after them in the way that I should, but I am never ever going to allow money to become my first objective in life."

The Emerging Principle of Interpersonal Relationships

After you've been around your group, invite them to try to collectively formulate some principles of interpersonal relationships. Some of these might evolve:

"I must never put positions above people. When I value things more than men and women, I am mixing up my values."

"I must learn that when a deep spiritual challenge comes, I must not let anything material come into my way and stop me from accepting it."

My Action Commitment

Invite each member of the group to make some commitment for the coming week. You might lead off with yours, which could be: "Instead of working overtime to gain more money as I had planned for next week, I am going to go visiting for the church and see if I can help someone discover spiritual values of life."

20

The One-Flesh Relationship

Scripture: Genesis 2:18-24; Ephesians 5:28-31

Psychodynamics

Marriage is the most intimate of all human relationships. It is so close that every defect in an individual's character soon becomes obvious to a spouse.

On the positive side, there are all sorts of benefits that come when two people team up together and learn to help each other.

Unfortunately, marriage also gives two people a built-in alibi for anything that happens in life. If something goes wrong, I can blame my spouse, and this can give me an escape from my personal responsibility.

We know, too, that in the interplay of this close relationship, it can become symbiotic, with a strong dominant male having a weak, yielding wife, or a talkative woman with a silent husband. Sometimes it can develop into a sado-masochistic experience, with one spouse becoming cruel and demanding while the other is yielding and willing to suffer.

With so many potentialities it is small wonder that many difficulties arise within marriages.

Background

Although we will be looking primarily at the passage from Genesis, there are actually three passages of Scripture which should be in our minds as we consider the one-flesh idea.

The Genesis passage presents a delightful picture of Adam in the Garden of Eden. The theme of this passage is that God provided a helpmeet for this lonely man. God said, "It is not good for man to be alone," and having caused a deep sleep to fall upon Adam, God took a rib from his side and created a wife for him.

A delighted Adam then said, "This is now bone of my bone and flesh of my flesh. She shall be called woman because she was taken out of man. Therefore shall a man leave his father and mother and cleave unto his wife, and they shall be one flesh."

Matthew Henry, commenting on this passage, said, "The woman was made out of a rib out of the side of Adam; not made out of his head to rule him; nor out of his feet to be trampled upon by him; but out of his side to be equal with him, under his arm to be protected, and near his heart to be loved."

The expression "one flesh" is used in the gospel story when the Pharisees have come to Jesus to try to trick him with a hypothetical situation about divorce. Jesus answered by reminding them of the original story about two people in marriage becoming "one flesh." He added, "What God hath joined together, let not man put asunder."

In the Ephesian epistle Paul takes up the idea of one flesh and gives it a unique twist. He urges husbands to love their wives, because in loving their wives, they really love themselves, since the two people are one flesh.

In summary, we might say the idea of one flesh has four implications:

1. *Marriage is commitment*—"What God hath joined together let not man put asunder."

2. *Marriage is an order of loyalties*—"For this cause shall a man leave his father and mother and cleave unto his wife."

3. *Marriage is a shared enterprise*—"It is not good for man to be alone. I will make a help meet for him."

4. *Marriage is self-love at its best*—"So ought men to love their wives as their own bodies. He that loveth his wife loveth himself."

The Sharing Session

The Bible Reading

You may preface the Bible reading segment with any of the

above information you feel will be helpful; then ask the group to pay particular attention to what they are reading.

The Reflection Period

Remind the group that marriage is probably the most widely experienced of all human relationships. Call their attention to the fact that we are concentrating on the idea of "one flesh."

Sharing Our Associations

Let us look in on Isabel Powell as she leads her group in sharing their associations. She begins by modeling, setting the example in the way in which she participates.

"These verses bring a flood of associations to me, and I'm going to have some difficulty in sorting them out.

"I guess that one association of the one flesh idea is the physical aspect of marriage. This has always been pretty important to me, but I suppose that in the final analysis I really see the physical as a mirror and image of the biblical idea of one flesh.

"In these days when divorce has become so easy, there have been times when, in my disappointment or petulance, I have wondered what it would be like to be free and unmarried again.

"The thought that most frequently comes to my mind is whether I could have ever won a Pulitzer prize. I was a journalism major in college, and one summer I worked for a newspaper. My boss often encouraged me and led me to believe I had potential, but I got married in my senior college year and, in rapid succession, had a couple of children.

"I have come to realize that this sort of reflection doesn't help me be a good wife. I have to go back to my commitment, remember that this is a permanent relationship, and be as creative as I can under the circumstances in which I find myself."

The Emerging Principle of Interpersonal Relationships

Encourage the group to reach a consensus about the principle of interpersonal relationships.

They might conclude:

"Because marriage is a life-long commitment, I should help people prepare carefully for it."

"Remembering the permanence of marriage, we should help people take actions which enrich their marriage relationship."

My Action Commitment

Isabel Powell can give the lead again: "I have resolved that I am not going to sit around lamenting a lost career and let it drive a wedge in my marriage. I might do some journalism on the side, but I'm going to be the best wife that I can."

21
Sharing

Scripture: Acts 2:41-47; 4:31-35

Psychodynamics

Possibly no single verse in the Bible has had so much influence on society as the one in our passage today which describes the way in which the early Christians shared everything, including their worldly goods. Many an idealist has quoted this statement to show the way in which men and women should learn to live with each other.

The eighteenth century saw communal colonies flourishing in the United States. It has been estimated that, at one time, as many as 100,000 people lived in over 100 such communities scattered across the country. The organization and practices of these groups indicated a great variety, but they all looked back to this verse as the authority for their existence.

In our own day, people as far removed from each other as the Hutterites, living industriously on their carefully cultivated farms, and the Children of God, residing in their makeshift quarters, have sought to emulate these early Christians.

Background

Today's Scripture passage must be considered against the background of the events that surrounded the day of Pentecost.

Following the descent of the Holy Spirit upon the infant church, the apostles preached with remarkable power, and 3,000 people were swept into the kingdom of God. In the midst of this high watermark of spiritual experience the early Christians became vividly aware of the experience of *koinonia*. This sharing spirit was so evident among these early Christians that they sold all their possessions and shared their worldly goods with each other.

We know little of this experiment except that it was apparently short-lived and seems to have been the material manifestation of an inward spirit of sharing.

Notice particularly the statement: "And they continued steadfastly in the apostle's doctrine and fellowship, and the breaking of bread and prayers." Fellowship was obviously a very important consideration in the early church. While it was important for them to understand the teachings of the church, participating in the Lord's Supper and praying were equally valuable for experiencing fellowship or *koinonia*.

The Sharing Session

The Bible Reading

You could begin by explaining that because today's lesson is about sharing, it might be a good idea to share in the reading of the Scriptures. So read the passage in unison.

The Reflection Period

Remind the group that sharing is the theme of the discussion today, and as we reflect on the passage, we should let our minds turn to the experiences of sharing.

Sharing Our Associations

Remember, we are not preaching sermons, we are encouraging the group to share. Don't let your group get involved in discussions about speaking in tongues or socialism or such issues.

Because of the potentialities of being sidetracked, it is doubly important that you model, so that the group will understand exactly what they are to do.

John Jackson models before his group, saying, "As I read this passage today, I was reminded of a sharing experience which meant very, very much to me.

"I have a close friend who believes in sharing, and one night he called and asked me if I would come to his house. When

I arrived, he had a funny-looking man sitting there with him. It turned out that this man was an alcoholic, and my friend was trying to help him quit blaming others for his misfortune and accept responsibility for himself.

"After we had talked for awhile, my friend said, 'Well, let's not waste time,' and turned to me and said, 'John, who are you?'

"I then proceeded to share some experiences from life in which I have been irresponsible. When I got through, the alcoholic man said, 'I want to share my experience,' and told us about the way in which he had spent his life blaming others, but now he was going to accept responsibility for himself. I learned that night that by sharing my experiences with other people, I can encourage them to share their experiences with me, and so I can help them in many ways."

The Emerging Principle of Interpersonal Relationships

In many ways this program is at the heart of the Christian's experiences of relationship. The group might make these formulations.

"God shared his love with men and women and we must share our love with our fellow believers."

"It is often easier to share our money with people than to share our experiences."

"I remember a saying I once heard, 'You cannot keep your experience unless you give it away.' Well, I'm determined I'm going to share my Christian experience with other people."

My Action Commitment

You might turn to the group and say, "In consideration of the Christian teaching about fellowship and sharing, I resolve that during this coming week,

"I will seek out some Christian who is lonely and spend some time sharing with him or her."

"When I go to church I will approach someone I have not spoken to before and introduce myself and try to share my faith."

leader's workshop

Maxims Frequently Used by Self-Help Groups

We have no perfect people in our groups. We have all failed at some point in our lives.

We are all strugglers together in the sea of life.

We acknowledge our own failures before we discuss the weaknesses of others.

We do not confess for others, but we concentrate on our own shortcomings.

A man is never stronger than when he is admitting his weaknesses.

We cannot accept good reasons for bad behavior.

We alone can do it, but we cannot do it alone.

Act as if . . .

It is much easier to act yourself into a new way of feeling than to feel yourself into a new way of acting.

We can't stop feeling, but we can direct behavior.

Do the thing and the rewards will emerge.

Our good deeds are our psychic assets, while our irresponsible acts are our liabilities.

We have no spectators, only participators.

Don't sit near the fire if your head is made of butter.

You can't help it if the birds fly over your head, but you can stop them from making a nest in your hair.

You didn't get into trouble overnight; you won't get out of it overnight.

Environment may have made you what you are, but you have no excuse to stay that way.

Becoming an open person is like peeling the skin of an onion, one layer at a time.

Do not nurse resentments; throw them out into the winter's night to the death they deserve.

22
A Forgiving Spirit

Scripture: Matthew 18:21-33

Psychodynamics

Most of us have two standards for faults and failures—one which we apply to ourselves, and another we use when we evaluate other people.

This is particularly so when we come to dealing with forgiveness. We expect people to be understanding with us, but when we in turn have to deal with others, we become very demanding. Yet we know we all make mistakes and could not exist without the understanding and acceptance of other people.

Background

The whole of this incident revolves around a question asked by the impulsive apostle, Peter. Peter, ever human, was aware of the problems of forgiveness and wanted to know if he should forgive his brother seven times. Jesus said he should forgive him seventy times seven.

Jesus then told the story of the man who, though forgiven much by his lord, nevertheless turned on his debtor and demanded full payment. The theme is obvious, that people who are forgiven should be willing to forgive others.

This is particularly so in the areas of home and family life.

The Sharing Session

The Bible Reading

Try a responsive reading today.

The Reflection Period

It might be a good idea today to have some background music for the reflection period. Why not try playing the music from the lovely hymn "Jesus Paid It All"? Or have someone sing it as a solo; then allow the thirty-second silence while the group concentrates on the message of the passage.

Sharing Our Associations

Lyndon Usher is conducting the group. He introduces himself to them. "This is going to be a particularly difficult subject for me to handle today. As your leader, I am expected to tell you the associations that come to my mind. Unfortunately, I'm having a battle to bring myself to do this, but I'll do the best I can to tell you what they are.

"When I think of forgiveness, I think of my father. He was a very cruel man. He treated my mother very badly. I can remember some horrible scenes in our home.

"When it came time for me to go to college, he told me that there was no sense in spending money on my education. So I went off to school and tried to make it through by myself. While I was there, I used the memory of his cruelty at home as a reason why I should goof off. I never did as well in college as I ought to have done. However, I had a convenient scapegoat and always placed the blame on my father.

"Then along came Valery. I fell for Valery the first moment I looked upon her. As the months went by and I courted her, I discovered that she was a very keen Christian. She encouraged me to go to church, and one night when the invitation was given, I went forward.

"I really entered into my Christian commitment and felt how wonderful it was to be forgiven by God. However, I still refused to forgive my father.

"My mother died of cancer. At the funeral I couldn't bear to go up and talk to my father. I felt that he had been so cruel to her and unkind to me.

"Valery has often urged me to think in a different way about Daddy, and I have tried but have not succeeded. I think that today I see why, and I know that if I'm really going to rejoice in the forgiveness that Christ has given me, I have to forgive him."

The Emerging Principle of Interpersonal Relationships

Have the group work on formulating this principle. Some of their opinions might be:

"If I say I am a Christian and my sins are forgiven, I must forgive somebody else."

"Our relationship to God and our relationship to our fellows have certain similarities, one of which is that as God forgave us, we must forgive them."

The Action Answer

This might be the time to spend around the commitment book. Are there members of the group that have refused to forgive someone? This might be the time for them to do something about it.

23
In-laws or Outlaws

Scripture: Ruth 1:1-18

Psychodynamics

Life is a web of relationships, and as the human grows, he moves into ever-widening experiences of affiliation. After the process of childhood and adolescence, the decision to marry brings in a whole new era.

There are relationship experiences within the marriage itself—husband-wife, parent-child—but the most sensitive of all is the in-law relationship, which stems from grafting two families to each other.

Many of the problems are peculiar to the ties involved. One study has shown that the man's mother was frequently the greatest threat to the relationship. She who loved her son and wanted the best for him wondered whether his new bride could manage the situation. So she interfered, and this interference brought trouble, often alienating her from the son whom she loved.

The bride's mother has not been altogether blameless. She wants to be sure of the breadwinner with whom her daughter has linked her life. Her doubts are seen in the aphorism, "Behind every successful man, there stands an astonished mother-in-law."

As in all relationships, verbal communication is of the utmost importance. If the "in-laws" get the feeling they are wanted only as baby sitters, they need to speak up. If the young people feel their in-laws are visiting too frequently or making too many demands, they should be open about it.

In any case, the relative should be the channel of communication. If the man's mother is giving the trouble, he should talk to her. On the other hand, should the wife's mother be the source of irritation, the wife is obviously the one to take up the matter.

Background

The book of Ruth is set in a rugged and turbulent period of Israel's history. Its setting is a pastoral scene and depicts how, in the midst of battles and conflicts and disorders, there is always a gentler side of life in which men love, work, weep, and laugh.

In many ways the book of Ruth is a strange story. It tells of the departure of Naomi and her family from Judah to the Gentile country of Moab to escape the scourge of famine. Tragedy dogged Naomi's footsteps: first, her husband died, then her two boys, Mahlon and Chilion, departed from the tenets of their religion and married Gentile girls. After both sons died, the distraught mother turned her face toward Jerusalem. Her dutiful daughters-in-law gathered their meager possessions and went with her.

The moment of drama came as they stood on the border of Judah. Naomi, with nothing to offer her daughters-in-law save sorrow and disappointment, turned to them and bade them return to their own land. Orpah saw the sense of it, but Ruth refused to go. Her immortal statement has retained its poignant message through the years: "Intreat me not to leave thee, or to return from following after thee: for whither thou goest, I will go; and where thou lodgest, I will lodge; thy people shall be my people, and thy God my God" (Ruth 1:16).

The relationship of Ruth and Naomi provides a picture of the ideal mother and daughter-in-law relationship

The Sharing Session

The Bible Reading

Watch out for the Scripture passage today. It has a number of proper names that may cause some stumbling for the inexperienced reader. Make sure you understand the pronunciations yourself, so you'll be able to help.

Reflection Period

Lead off by modeling.

When Bob Pringle sat down with his group, he stated, "When I read about a mother-in-law, I see red. I sometimes wonder if there are any good mothers-in-law.

"My mother-in-law has always been a Nosey Parker. As soon as we met, she started quizzing me about my job and my prospects and whether I had a savings account.

"It always seemed to me that she was pushing Harriet—that's my wife—to push me. She talked us into buying a house, and she was forever coming up with suggestions about the fence and the yard and what painting needed to be done. She sometimes acted as if it was her house rather than ours.

"I am so sensitive that the moment she mentions something, I take the opposite position; I think the psychologists called that contra-suggestion. I know Harriet often finds herself in a very difficult and awkward position as she becomes the go-between.

"In my more rational moments I can see that she really has helped us, and I guess I'm going to have to spend some time on building a better relationship with her.

"I realize, too, that Harriet is all she has. All her life is wrapped up in Harriet, and it is rather unfortunate that I expect Harriet to give me more attention so that she cannot spend so much time with her mother."

The Emerging Principle of Interpersonal Relationships

Encourage the group to form some principles for relating to in-laws. These might include:

"I can treat my in-laws in the same way I treat my friends. If friends offer advice, I accept or reject it without feeling antagonistic to them."

"My in-laws gave me my spouse. I will always be under a debt of gratitude to them."

"I will be an in-law myself one day, and I am going to try to treat my in-laws the way I would want to be treated later myself."

My Action Commitment

Some commitments that might be made:

"I am going to take time to sit down and talk with my mother-in-law."

"My mother-in-law has been keeping house for many years. I'm going to ask her about her recipes and some hints about how I can run my house more efficiently."

"I'm going to invite Jim's mother over to have a meal so that she will get the impression that we don't just want her when we want her to do something for us."

24

What We See in Others

Scripture: 2 Samuel 12:1-13

Psychodynamics

Most people have two standards of behavior, one for their own behavior and an entirely different one for the behavior of others. Much of this attitude comes from a psychological mechanism, which some psychologists call *projection*, a technique by which a person sees his own faults dramatized in the actions of other people. Consequently, he has a tendency to condemn in other people what he dislikes in himself.

It is extremely difficult to look at ourselves objectively. As the famous Scottish poet, Burns, said:

> O wad some power the giftie gie us
> To see oursels as others see us!
> It wad frae monie a blunder free us.

Background

In many ways this story demonstrates the technique of Experiential Bible Study. You might say that the prophet Nathan used a technique similar to what we use in our week-by-week sessions.

The story of Nathan and David finds the Hebrew king at his worst. He had just passed through the tragic maneuvering of Uriah to have him killed in battle. David was thus able to move in and take Bathsheba as his wife.

When Nathan appeared before David's court, he made a tactful approach to the king, by telling a story of a rich man and a poor man. The poor man owned one little ewe lamb, which was his children's pet; he fed it from his own plate and cuddled it as if it were his child.

On one occasion, when the rich man had a visitor in his home, instead of killing one of his own flock, he took the poor man's one little lamb and butchered it to prepare a meal for his guest.

As David listened to the story, he was moved by the patent unfairness of it all, and he blazed in indignation and declared that the man guilty of such a heinous offense would be punished.

Then came the dramatic moment, as Nathan zeroed in to make the application, saying, "Thou art the man." Then he pointed out how David the king had destroyed Uriah to gain possession of his wife.

The Sharing Session

Bible Reading

Since this story is so well known in the King James Version, you will not need a modern translation to catch its meaning and drama.

Reflection Period

Point out to your group the technique that Nathan used in the way he presented the story to David and had David associate with it. You could also indicate that David missed the point and failed to make the application to himself. Ask the members of your group to beware of this possibility and to make a personal application.

Sharing Our Associations

Henrietta Kent is leading her group and says, "As you know, I have two teenage children, and I am coming to believe that adolescents bring the supreme test to adults' mental health.

"I've always been worried about all the talk concerning drugs, and I am forever warning the kids about how dangerous they are.

"Then, one might John came home late, and I smelled this sweet sort of odor on him, and I began to wonder if he were smoking pot.

"Well I challenged him, and he denied it, but he became very sassy and said, "I don't really think you have any right to speak to me about pot.

"When I asked why, he answered, 'Well, you're a social drinker and more. I notice the way you've got to have a drink every time you're under stress. As I hear it, alcohol is the worst drug of all, and you've got the nerve to tell me to keep away from drugs.'

"That sure hit me in the eye. Here I was checking up on my kids, and I needed to do something about myself.

"As I associate with this passage, I've come to see that I'd better be careful about what I criticize in other people, if I do not pay attention to what I am doing myself."

The Emerging Principle of Interpersonal Relationships

Help the group formulate a principle: "When I see something I object to in others, I should ask myself if I am innocent in this area of my behavior."

My Action Commitment

I am going to spend more time looking at myself and my own behavior than in criticizing others. If I see something in others that annoys me, I will pay attention to that matter in my own life.

25

Hi, Neighbor!

Scripture: Luke 10:30-37

Psychodynamics

America was shocked some years ago by the murder of Kitty Genovese. Over thirty people heard her cries for help, but no one raised a finger to do anything about it. When asked why they had not done anything, the standard reply was, "We didn't want to get involved."

This attitude is a sad commentary on the detachment of modern man from his fellows, and it sounds more like the law of the jungle than the highly developed twentieth-century civilization.

It is certainly not the Christian attitude toward men and women. We are to help our fellowman, and what hurts him also hurts us. It is certainly not the attitude of the great preacher-poet, John Donne, who said, "No man is an island, entire of itself; every man is a piece of the continent, a part of the main; if a clod be washed away by the sea, Europe is the less, as well as if a promontory were, as well as if a manor of thy friends or of thine own were; any man's death diminishes me, because I am involved in mankind; and therefore never send to know for whom the bell tolls; it tolls for thee."

Background

You should know something about the antagonism between the Jews and the Samaritans. The Samaritans were a group of people who, while they lived within the boundaries of Palestine, were nevertheless quite different from the orthodox Jews.

The Samaritan religion was an aberration of Judaism with such distortions that orthodox Jews looked upon the Samaritans with contempt.

All of this makes the biblical incident of the Good Samaritan much more vivid in its application.

The story Jesus told was provoked by the question of an expert in the Jewish law to whom Jesus had said that the all-important thing was to love our neighbor. The question that the man shot back to our Lord was "Who is my neighbor?"

Jesus answered this question with a story. The story he told was of a traveler who was robbed on his way from Jerusalem to Jericho. The thieves left him in bad shape on the side of the road.

Then came a priest and Levite, both members of the orthodox Jewish faith, but they passed by on the other side of the road.

The climax came with the arrival of the despised Samaritan. He took the man, doctored him, and arranged for him to be cared for in a hostel.

While the orthodox Jews did nothing to help their fellow Jew, the man who had such strange beliefs stopped to share his worldly goods and to help the stranger who needed assistance.

Scripture Reading

This passage is so familiar that you will probably make the message more effective by having it read from a modern translation. Other group members could follow in their own Bibles.

The Reflection Period

Remind your group of the danger of familiarity breeding contempt. Because we have heard the passage so many times, we may easily overlook its spiritual significance. Urge the group members to let their minds run free and try to associate with what is going on in this passage.

Sharing Our Associations

John Saunders is leading his group. He says, "When I think of this passage, my mind goes back to the day when a preacher was driving me down the road in the mountains of West Virginia.

He had picked me up at the airport, and I was weary from the journey. I was eagerly anticipating getting some rest before I began the conference for that evening.

"As we drove, the preacher pointed to some skid marks running off at the side of the road and said, 'It looks to me as if a car might have gone over here.'

"As soon as the car stopped, he jumped out and scrambled down the slope. I was vaguely irritated. I wanted to get to my room. Nevertheless, I jumped out and scrambled after him.

"When we got to the bottom we found an automobile turned over, and under it, two women and a baby. We finally got them out of the car.

When I got back to my room, I had a horrible reaction as I thought of what might have happened if the preacher hadn't gone to help. I was also vividly aware of my attitude, that I was unwilling to inconvenience myself because I was tired, yet here were people in great need of my assistance."

The Emerging Principle of Interpersonal Relationships

The principle that emerges here could be, "My actions always affect other people. No one can remain uninvolved."

My Action Commitment

Some of the action commitments that might be made would include such things as these:

"I am going to pull my weight in the situations in life."

"I will work more diligently at both my church and my civic commitments."

"When I face a difficult situation next week, I am going to be prepared to go the extra mile."

26
Fed Up with Home

Scripture: Luke 15:11-25

Psychodynamics

This is the classical drama of family life and raises some of the most complex problems of that venerable institution.

How could two boys who grow up in the same family turn out so differently? Why did the younger boy become so dissatisfied with his home life? What about the difference in attitudes between the two boys? The other boy was conscientious but had a bad spirit, and the other boy, who had been in revolt against his home, returned with a contrite spirit.

All of these problems emerge in one of the greatest dramas of all literature.

Background

This whole chapter is the record of lost things—a piece of silver, a sheep, and a boy. Notice the way in which they were lost. A piece of silver rolled away, the sheep, nibbling grass, wandered away, but the boy deliberately made his choice and wrenched himself loose from his family.

The Sharing Session

The Bible Reading

This is the drama of two men, the prodigal and his father. Try introducing the reading by saying, "As the story today has to do with two men, we will have two men to read the passage alternatively to us."

The Reflection Period

Remind the group of the familiarity of this passage. This may be either an asset or a liability. Warn them not to theologize but to seek to identify a personal relationship with the characters in the story.

Sharing Our Associations

Bill Huntsucker is conducting his group, and he models.

"I have no problem in identifying with this passage today. I grew up in a Christian home, and when I went into the service, I saw it as an opportunity to try the things I'd heard the other guys talking about. I certainly did try most of the things that were available, and they left ashes in my mouth.

"But when I came home again, I revolted when my mother asked me if I were going to church. I was really ugly with her, and I know that I hurt her, but I felt that she was trying to dominate me.

"I surely felt miserable in the days that followed. All the others in the family were going to church, and I was spending my time with some guys I knew my mother would disapprove of.

"Then my sister invited me over to her house. She and her husband went all out to make me feel at home, and I gradually got into the habit of spending all my spare time with them. Naturally I went along to church with them.

"Mother died later, and I'm afraid I'll always have a memory of how stupid I was in my revolt against what I imagined was her domination."

The Emerging Principle of Interpersonal Relationships

Some of the principles might be:

"It is often more difficult to relate well to members of the family than to outsiders."

"In a family group we live so close that little things which would not be noticed in other settings become sources of irritation."

"Being a good family member requires work and effort."

My Action Commitment

This is a sensitive area of human experience, and many people are aware of their need to do something about their family relationships. Some of the commitments that they might make are: "I will spend more time working on relationships within my family."

"I'm going to tell my parents how much I appreciate them while I still have them with me."

"I am going to set about to be as nice to my family members as I am to people outside my family that I try to impress."

Epilog

How did you like this series of programs? Did you sense the response of people who, perhaps for the first time, were applying the Scriptures to their lives?

Now that you have learned the technique, why not go ahead and work up some programs of your own?